Our Hymns of Praise

OUR HYMNS OF PRAISE

J. Mark Stauffer, *Editor*

Illustrations by
Esther Rose Graber

HERALD PRESS
Scottdale, Pennsylvania/Kitchener, Ontario

Acknowledgments

A number of years ago the Music Committee of Mennonite General Conference asked Karl Massanari and Mary Royer, both of Goshen, Ind., and Elsie Martin, of Harrisonburg, Va., to begin work on a songbook for young children. The report of this subcommittee, dated July 1, 1950, was a productive one. It contained guiding principles and a list of songs. Following this the work was carried forward by the editor of the Music Committee. God has helped us with our task.

This publication represents the generous labors of the Music Committee of Mennonite General Conference: Walter E. Yoder, Chairman; J. Mark Stauffer, Secretary; John P. Duerksen, Paul Erb, Chester K. Lehman, Earl M. Maust, and Dwight Weldy. We wish also to express appreciation to Esther Rose Graber, artist; Nancy Burkholder, writer of music parts; Mrs. M. T. Brackbill, Helen Trumbo, Paul M. Lederach, C. B. Shoemaker, Ellrose D. Zook, and others who gave valuable counsel.

We wish also to acknowledge with grateful appreciation the kind co-operation of individuals and publishers who have granted permission for the use of copyrighted songs. An earnest effort was made to ascertain the copyright status of each song. Should any songs be included without proper permission and credit, the publisher will upon notification gladly make necessary corrections.

OUR HYMNS OF PRAISE

Copyright © 1958 by Herald Press, Scottdale, Pa. 15683
   Published simultaneously in Canada by Herald Press,
   Kitchener, Ont. N2G 4M5
International Standard Book Number: 0-8361-1126-5
Printed in the United States of America

Fourth Printing, 1977

Preface

Make a joyful noise unto the Lord, all ye lands.
Serve the Lord with gladness:
Come before his presence with singing.
—Psalm 100:1, 2.

Singing has always been a part of worship, and congregational a cappella singing has found an important place in the worship of the church. One of the finest ways to promote a cappella congregational singing is to teach young children to sing good sacred music. Children can learn early to appreciate sacred music and to express their worship in singing with the congregation, with the family, and with other groups. It is the purpose of this book to help lead children into the experience of worship through singing.

The songs in this book have been selected for primary and junior children of grades one to six, ages six to eleven. Teachers of young children will find these songs useful in Christian day school, summer Bible school, Sunday school, Sunday evening service, home, and in choral groups composed of young children.

The tunes of the songs represent the best works of many composers of children's music. The melodies are easily adapted to children's voices and appeal to children's appreciation of beauty.

The words express praise and thanksgiving to God for His world and loving care; they tell the story of the life of Jesus, the children's best Friend; they tell about the Bible; they express love to others; and they suggest prayers in children's language.

Lead children to interpret and express these songs so that their singing experiences will be worship experiences.

1. Be sure you are singing each song correctly, both melody and rhythm. Use a small, informal conducting pattern.

2. Sing in a personal, friendly manner. Your voice should be light and clear. Do not use your full, mature voice. Sing with a mezzo-voice (half voice).

3. In teaching young children to sing, use the rote method. Sing the song two or three times in a clear, simple manner. Then invite the children to sing with you. Begin to withdraw your voice as soon as possible. The rule is: "Sing for your children, not with them." Depending on the age of the children and the length of the song, you may want to teach the song by phrases.

4. There are one-, two-, and three-part songs in this book. When learning songs with more than one part, and if your children are old enough and the group large enough, let the lighter, higher voices sing the melody and the other voices sing with an adult who is able to carry the other part or parts.

5. Listen for the child who has not found his singing voice. He will probably sing in a conversational manner. *He is not a monotone.* A little special understanding and ear-training experience will help him to sing correctly. Calling the class roll by singing the child's first name, using the interval 5 - 3 (sol - mi), is excellent. The child is to match your interval by singing, "I'm here."

6. The singing range for young children is limited to the outer lines of the G clef (e - f). A few songs in this book will need to be transposed upward to satisfy this standard. Use a pitch instrument to secure proper pitch.

7. A child's voice is delicate. Do not spoil his voice by asking a child to sing

too high or too low. Do not ask him to sing loud; let him sing free and easy. Do not ask him to sing too long. The singing period should not exceed fifteen minutes unless the songs are interspersed with other inspirational features.

8. The poorer singer should be placed beside or in front of a good singer. As a general rule, the most talented singers should be placed in the back of the group.

9. Good singing cannot exist or develop amid disorder and confusion. Quietness and attention must prevail before children can sing.

10. The teacher should feel free to move around among the children while they are singing. Sing softly with the musically dependent child. Create an informal singing atmosphere.

11. Help the children to appreciate the meaning of what they sing. Songs about God's world and seasons will interest children who have collected leaves and wondered at their different patterns, who have watched the stars at night, and who have read nature stories. Songs about His love and care will be understandable to children who have pets and who know a happy home life. "Saviour, Like a Shepherd Lead Us" will speak to a child who has just heard how shepherds care for their sheep. Lead the children to express the central feeling of each song. Are you singing a prayer song? Then sing quietly and reverently. Are you singing a happy praise song? Then sing brightly.

Remember, you are training the future church to sing. God is interested in your task. He will help you to achieve. To this end may the Lord bless our labors in this common cause.

—J. Mark Stauffer.

Contents

GOD, OUR FATHER
- *Praise to Him*
  - I Will Sing to the Lord 13
  - Praise Him, Praise Him 14
  - Come, We That Love the Lord 14
  - Come with Hearts Rejoicing 15
  - Heavenly Father 15
  - Oh, Worship the King 16
  - We, Thy People, Praise Thee 16
- *His World and Seasons*
  - Sing to God 18
  - Little Birds Are Gaily Singing 18
  - And God Said 19
  - God Made the Beautiful Sunshine 19
  - He Doeth All Things Well 20
  - Who Made the Pretty Lilies? 21
  - All Things Bright and Beautiful (First Tune) 22
  - All Things Bright and Beautiful (Second Tune) 23
  - This Is My Father's World 25
  - All Creatures of Our God and King 26
  - Smiles of Our Father 27
  - Happy Thought 27
  - See the Shining Dewdrops 29
  - Wind, Sun, and Rain 29
  - We Thank Thee 30
  - A Springtime Prayer 31
  - 'Tis God Who Sends the Spring 31
  - Summertime 32
  - Autumn 32
  - Praise to God, Immortal Praise 33
  - Winter Song 35
  - Another Year Is Dawning 35
  - Father, We Bring Thee Our Praises 36

- *Thanksgiving for His Love and Care*
  - God Loves Me 36
  - God Sees the Little Sparrow Fall 37
  - Praise and Thanks 38
  - Sing to God in Joyful Voice 39
  - Great Things 39
  - Faithful Is God 40
  - Thou Art with Us 41
  - Thanking God 41
  - Thy Mercies, Lord 42
  - Praise Him 42
  - Praise to God for Things We See 43
  - Can a Little Child like Me? 44
  - We Thank Thee, Father, for Our Homes 45
  - We Thank Thee, Loving Father 46
  - A Child's Prayer (I) 46
  - Lord, I Would Own Thy Tender Care 47
  - We Give Thanks 47
  - Father, Hear Thy Children Sing 48
  - The Prayer of the Children 48
  - For the Beauty of the Earth 49
- *Prayer to Him*
  - Prayer for Peace 50
  - Hear Our Prayer, O Lord 51
  - Father, Teach Me 51
  - Father, Lead Me Day by Day 52
  - Lord, Teach a Little Child to Pray 52
  - A Child's Prayer (II) 53
  - Thank You, God, for All I Have 53
  - Teach Us to Pray 54

JESUS, OUR SAVIOUR
- *His Birth and Childhood (Christmas)*
  - The First Christmas Night 55
  - Bethlehem 57
  - O Little Town of Bethlehem 58

Welcome, Holy Night 59
Silent Night 60
Baby Jesus 61
Little Baby Jesus 61
Away in a Manger (First Tune) 62
Away in a Manger (Second Tune) 63
O Come, Little Children 64
Christmas Chorale 65
Cradled upon a Bed of Hay 66
Mary's Lullaby 66
Lullaby to the Christ Child 67
Shepherds Leave the Hillside 67
Stars Were Gleaming 69
The Holy Child 70
Shepherds, Shake Off Your Drowsy Sleep 70
Christmas Carol 71
Carol, Children, Carol 73
We Three Kings of Orient Are 74
Happy Christmas Day 75
Glory to God in the Highest 76
Infant So Gentle 76
Joy to the World 77
Now Let Your Happy Voices Ring 78
Thou Holy Christ-Child, Blest and Dear 78
When Jesus Was a Little Boy 79
In the Temple 80

His Life and Love
Jesus Loves Me 81
Jesus Loves Even Me 82
O, We, the Little Children 83
Jesus Is the Friend of Children 83
The Children's Friend 84
Once upon a Hillside 84
That Sweet Story of Old 85
Tell Me the Stories of Jesus 86
Gracious Saviour, Gentle Shepherd ... 87
Saviour, like a Shepherd Lead Us 88

His Death and Resurrection
Let Me Learn of Jesus 87
God's Love Eternal 89
There Is a Green Hill Far Away 90

At the Dawn of Easter Day 91
Alleluia! Easter Angels 91
Christ the Lord Is Ris'n Today 93
Now Let Us All with One Accord 93
Jesus, from Thy Throne on High 94
There Is a Happy Land 94
Jewels 95

Prayer and Praise to Him
Lord, Who Lovest Little Children 96
A Prayer to Jesus 96
My Jesus, I Love Thee 97
Fairest Lord Jesus 98
All Glory, Laud and Honor 99
"Hosanna!" Be the Children's Song .. 100
Little Children, Praise the Saviour ... 100

Serving Jesus
I Would Follow Jesus 102
A Child's Prayer (III) 103
All for Jesus, All for Jesus 103
Anywhere with Jesus 104
Two Little Hands 105
I Give Thee My Hands 106

THE BIBLE
Book Divine 106
For Stories Fine and True 106
The Bible Helps Me 107
Little Moses 108
Dare to Be a Daniel 108

SUNDAY WORSHIP
Happy Hearts 110
I Was Glad When They Said unto Me .. 110
This Is the Day the Lord Hath Made 111
When to Church I Go 111
Enter into His Gates 113
Praise the Lord 113
We Love Our Church, O God 114
Here in Our Father's House 114
How Lovely Are the Messengers 115
Thy Work, O God, Needs Many Hands 115
Heavenly Father, We Thy Children ... 117

We Bring to Thee Our Offerings 117
Closing Prayer 118
May the Grace of Christ, Our Saviour 118

LOVE TO OTHERS
Father and Mother
To Thy Father and Thy Mother 119
Honor Thy Father and Mother 119
Home 121
Mother's Day 121

Friends We Know
Love One Another 122
The Golden Rule 122
Little Things 123
God Wants Us to Be Cheerful 124

Friends Far Away
We Are All God's Little Children 125
We Pray for Children O'er the Sea 125
God's World 126
Once Again, Dear Lord, We Pray 126
The Many, Many Children 127
True Neighbors 128

MORNING SONGS
Thanksgiving
Thanksgiving 128
Morning Prayer (I) 129
God's Gift of Day and Night 129
Thanks to God 130
Children's Chorale 130
Morning Hymn (I) 131
Morning Hymn (II) 133

Thanksgiving and Petition
Morning Prayer (II) 133
Father, We Thank Thee (First Tune) 134
Father, We Thank Thee (Second Tune) 135
Morning Song 135
I Thank Thee, Lord, for Quiet Rest 136
A Hymn of Thanks 136
Prayer for Each Day 137

A Child's Prayer (IV) 137
O God, I Thank Thee for Each Sight .. 138

Petition
The Morning Bright 138
Now I Wake 139
Morning Prayer (III) 139
Prayer 140
Now the Shades of Night Are Gone 141
Father, Hear Thy Little Children 141
Morning Praise 142
Our Father, As We Start the Day 142
God's Love 143

EVENING SONGS
The Good Shepherd 145
Evening 145
God Our Father Watch Will Keep 146
Evening Prayer 146
Day Is Done 147
Now the Day Is Over 149
Dear Father, Bless Each Little Child 149
A Child's Prayer (V) 150
An Evening Hymn 150
A Child's Evensong 151
Jesus, Tender Shepherd, Hear Me
  (First Tune) 153
Jesus, Tender Shepherd, Hear Me
  (Second Tune) 153
When I Say My Prayer 154
Evening Hymn 155

TABLE SONGS
My Prayer 155
For Health and Strength 157
Choral Grace 157
Thank Thee, Heav'nly Father 158
Thank You, God 158

LULLABIES
Hush, My Babe 159
Slumber Song 161

Praise Him, Praise Him

Anonymous   Arranged by Hubert P. Main

1. Praise Him, praise Him, all ye lit-tle chil-dren, God is love, God is love;
2. Love Him, love Him, all ye lit-tle chil-dren, God is love, God is love;
3. Thank Him, thank Him, all ye lit-tle chil-dren, God is love, God is love;
4. Serve Him, serve Him, all ye lit-tle chil-dren, God is love, God is love;

Praise Him, praise Him, all ye lit-tle chil-dren, God is love, God is love.
Love Him, love Him, all ye lit-tle chil-dren, God is love, God is love.
Thank Him, thank Him, all ye lit-tle chil-dren, God is love, God is love.
Serve Him, serve Him, all ye lit-tle chil-dren, God is love, God is love.

From *Songs for Preschool Children*. Copyright, 1926, by The Standard Publishing Company.

Come, We That Love the Lord

Isaac Watts   George Frederick Handel

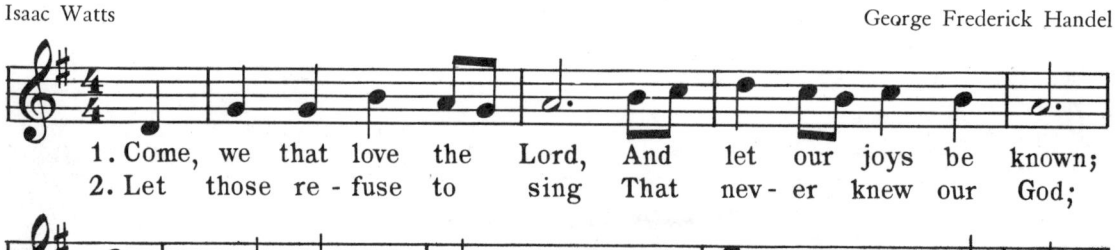

1. Come, we that love the Lord, And let our joys be known;
2. Let those re-fuse to sing That nev-er knew our God;

Join in a song with sweet ac-cord And thus sur-round the throne.
But chil-dren of the heav-'nly King May speak their joys a-broad.

From *Music Hour*, Book II. Used by special permission of Silver Burdett Company, New York.

Come with Hearts Rejoicing

Lina A. Rauschenberg
Arranged from Beethoven by Lina A. Rauschenberg

Words and music copyright, 1938, by Lina A. Rauschenberg. Used by special permission.

Heavenly Father

Salisbury Collection
Felix Mendelssohn-Bartholdy

From *Music Hour*, Book IV. Used by special permission of Silver Burdett Company, New York.

Oh, Worship the King

R. H. Grant
Arr. from Michael Haydn

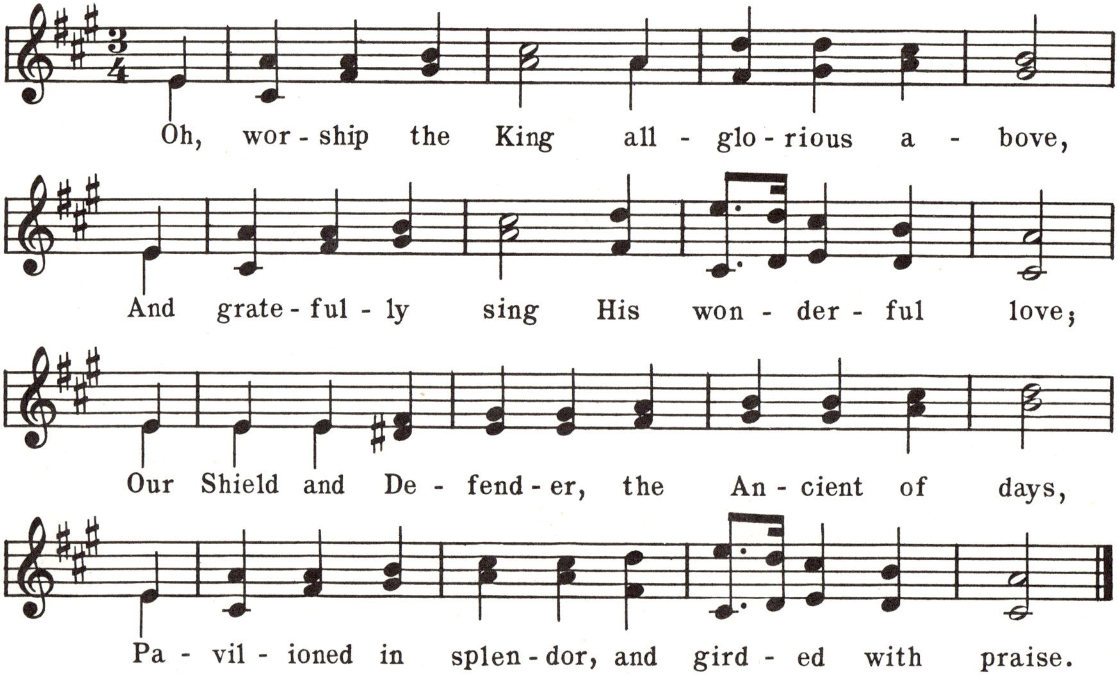

Oh, wor-ship the King all - glo-rious a - bove,
And grate-ful-ly sing His won-der-ful love;
Our Shield and De-fend-er, the An-cient of days,
Pa - vil - ioned in splen-dor, and gird - ed with praise.

We, Thy People, Praise Thee

Kate Stearns Page
Arranged from Franz Joseph Haydn

1. & 2. We, Thy peo-ple, praise Thee, praise Thee, God of ev-ery na-tion!

From *Singing Worship* by Edith Lovell Thomas. Abingdon-Cokesbury Press. Words used by permission of G. Schirmer, Inc. Music used by permission of Edith Lovell Thomas.

Sing to God

Adapted
Joseph Pleyl

1. Chant thanks-giv-ing, march a-long, Lift-ing hearts on wings of song!
2. Sing to God, the heav'n-ly King, Let our voic-es proud-ly ring!

Giv-ing thanks for hap-py days, Sing we our Cre-a-tor's praise.
Sing our great Cre-a-tor's praise, Glo-rious all His works and ways.

From *The American Singer*, Book IV, by Beattie and Wolverton. Used by permission of American Book Company.

Little Birds Are Gaily Singing

E. Hare
French Folk Tune

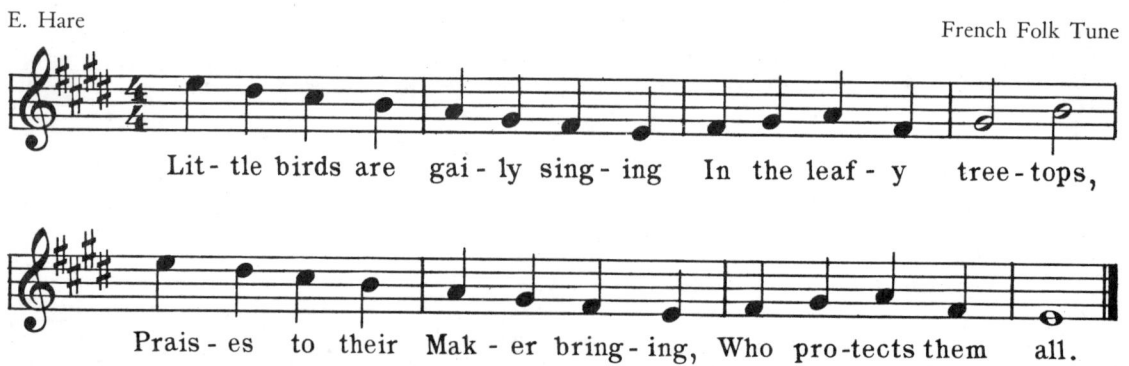

Lit-tle birds are gai-ly sing-ing In the leaf-y tree-tops,

Prais-es to their Mak-er bring-ing, Who pro-tects them all.

From Music Reader *for Lutheran Schools*. Used by permission of Concordia Publishing House.

And God Said

Mrs. James W. Wood

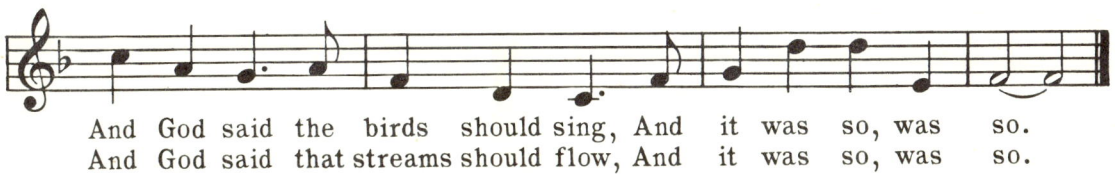

1. And God said the sun should shine, The rain should fall, the flowers should grow,
2. And God said the grass should grow, The trees bear fruit, the winds should blow,

And God said the birds should sing, And it was so, was so.
And God said that streams should flow, And it was so, was so.

From *Service in Song,* by Johnnie B. Wood. Used by permission.

God Made the Beautiful Sunshine

M.A. Mildred Adair

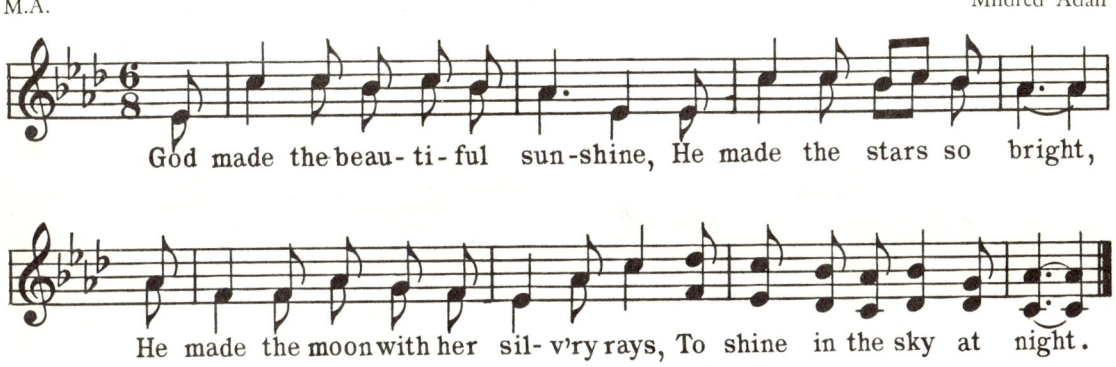

God made the beau-ti-ful sun-shine, He made the stars so bright,

He made the moon with her sil-v'ry rays, To shine in the sky at night.

From *Songs for Preschool Children.* Copyright, 1926, by The Standard Publishing Company.

He Doeth All Things Well

Elizabeth Cushing Taylor   W. Lawrence Curry

1. God, who made the sun so bright, Made the moon to give us light,
2. God, who made the winds to blow, Made the grass and trees to grow,

Made the stars to shine at night, He do-eth all things well.
Made all things a-bove, be-low, He do-eth all things well.

Words and music from *When a Little Child Wants to Sing*, copyright, 1935, by the Presbyterian Board of Christian Education. Used by permission.

Who Made the Pretty Lilies?

Mrs. C. D. Martin   W. Stillman Martin

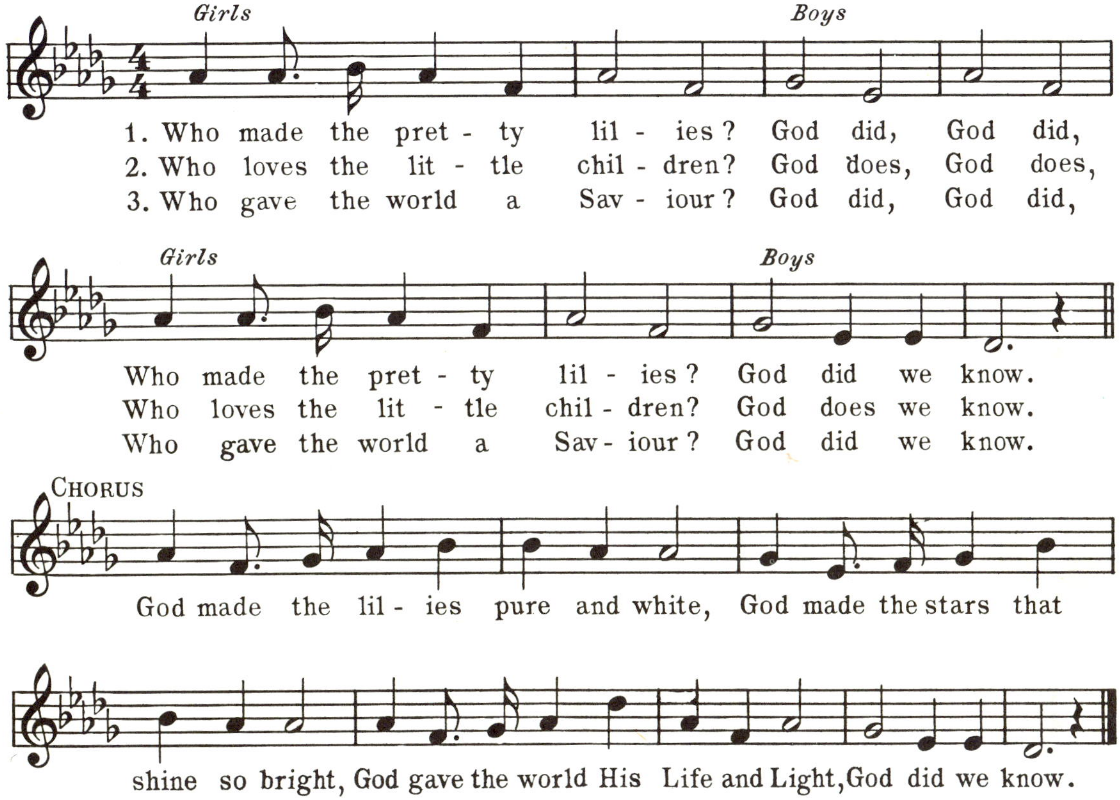

Girls   *Boys*

1. Who made the pret - ty lil - ies? God did, God did,
2. Who loves the lit - tle chil - dren? God does, God does,
3. Who gave the world a Sav - iour? God did, God did,

Girls   *Boys*

Who made the pret - ty lil - ies? God did we know.
Who loves the lit - tle chil - dren? God does we know.
Who gave the world a Sav - iour? God did we know.

Chorus

God made the lil - ies pure and white, God made the stars that shine so bright, God gave the world His Life and Light, God did we know.

Copyright, 1909, by Judefind Bros.

All Things Bright and Beautiful

Cecil Frances Alexander First Tune Adapted from a Danish Folk Song

1. Each lit-tle flower that o-pens, Each lit-tle bird that sings,
2. The pur-ple-head-ed moun-tain, The riv-er run-ning by,

God made their glow-ing col-ors, He made their ti-ny wings.
The sun-set and the morn-ing That bright-en up the sky.

Refrain

Yes, all things bright and beau-ti-ful, All crea-tures great and small,

And all things wise and won-der-ful, The Lord God made them all.

From *Songs for Little People*, by Danielson and Conant. Copyright, the Pilgrim Press. Used by permission.

All Things Bright and Beautiful

Cecil Frances Alexander • Second Tune • English Melody

All things bright and beau-ti-ful, All crea-tures great and small,

All things wise and won-der-ful, The Lord God made them all. *Fine*

1. Each lit-tle flower that o-pens, Each lit-tle bird that sings, God
2. The pur-ple-head-ed moun-tain, The riv-er run-ning by, The
3. The cold wind in the win-ter, The pleas-ant sum-mer sun, The
4. The tall trees in the green-wood, The mead-ows for our play, The
5. He gave us eyes to see them And lips that we might tell How

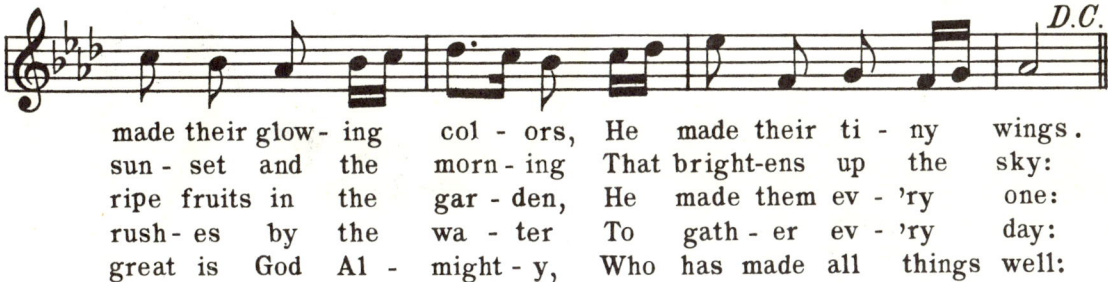

D.C.

made their glow-ing col-ors, He made their ti-ny wings.
sun-set and the morn-ing That bright-ens up the sky:
ripe fruits in the gar-den, He made them ev-'ry one:
rush-es by the wa-ter To gath-er ev-'ry day:
great is God Al-might-y, Who has made all things well:

By permission of J. Curwen & Sons Ltd., London.

This Is My Father's World

Maltbie D. Babcock
Franklin L. Sheppard

1. This is my Father's world, And to my list'ning ears, All nature sings, and round me rings The music of the spheres. This is my Father's world, I rest me in the thought Of rocks and trees, of skies and seas, His hand the wonders wrought.

2. This is my Father's world, The birds their carols raise, The morning light, the lily white, Declare their Maker's praise. This is my Father's world, He shines in all that's fair; In the rustling grass I hear Him pass, He speaks to me ev'ry-where.

All Creatures of Our God and King

Translated from the Hymn of St. Francis by W. H. Draper

1. All crea-tures of our God and King, Lift up your voice and with us sing,
2. Thou rush-ing wind that art so strong, Ye clouds that sail in heav'n a - long,
3. Thou flow-ing wa - ter, pure and clear, Make mu - sic for thy Lord to hear,

Al - le - lu - ia, Al - le - lu - ia. Thou burn-ing sun with gold - en beam,
O praise Him, O praise Him. Thou ris - ing morn in praise re - joice,
Al - le - lu - ia, Al - le - lu - ia. Thou fire, so mas - ter - ful and bright,

Thou sil - ver moon with soft - er gleam,
Ye lights of eve - ning find a voice, O praise Him, O praise Him,
That giv - est man both warmth and light,

Al - le - lu - ia, Al - le - lu - ia, Al - le - lu - ia.

Used by permission of J. Curwen & Sons Ltd.

Smiles of Our Father

L. C. Lockley
William J. Kraft

Smiles of our Father are sunshine and rain;
Let us re-pay Him and smile back a-gain.

From *Music Hour,* Book II. Used by special permission of Silver Burdett Company, New York.

Happy Thought

Robert Louis Stevenson
Arranged by Grace Wilbur Conant

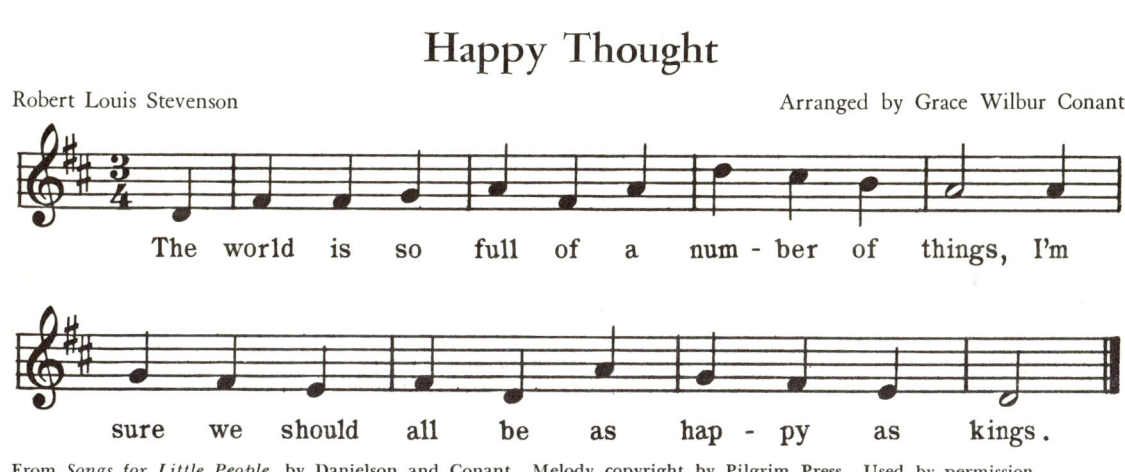

The world is so full of a number of things, I'm sure we should all be as happy as kings.

From *Songs for Little People,* by Danielson and Conant. Melody copyright by Pilgrim Press. Used by permission.

See the Shining Dewdrops

Anonymous
C. H. Rinck

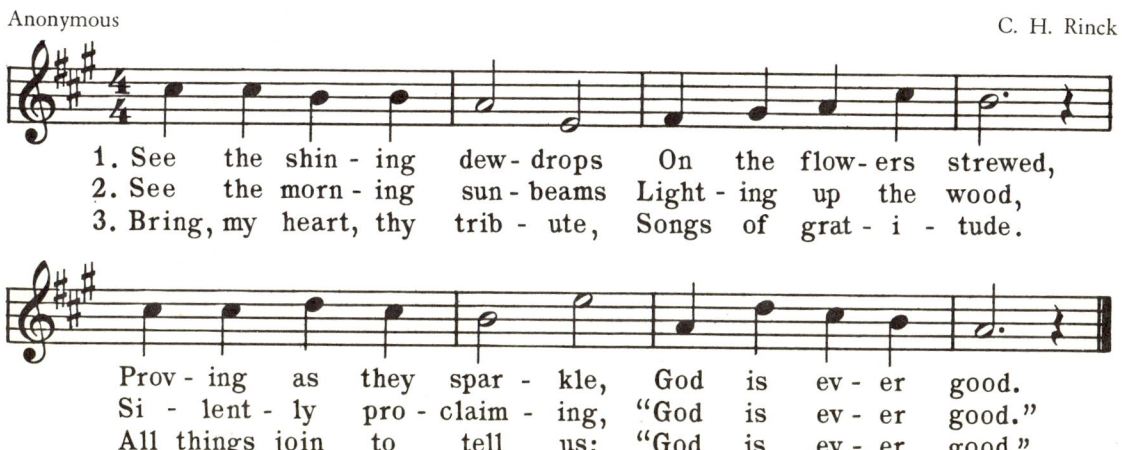

1. See the shin-ing dew-drops On the flow-ers strewed,
2. See the morn-ing sun-beams Light-ing up the wood,
3. Bring, my heart, thy trib-ute, Songs of grat-i-tude.

Prov-ing as they spar-kle, God is ev-er good.
Si-lent-ly pro-claim-ing, "God is ev-er good."
All things join to tell us: "God is ev-er good."

From MUSIC READER *for Lutheran Schools.* Used by permission of Concordia Publishing House.

Wind, Sun, and Rain

Ida F. Leyda
Emma Virginia Miller

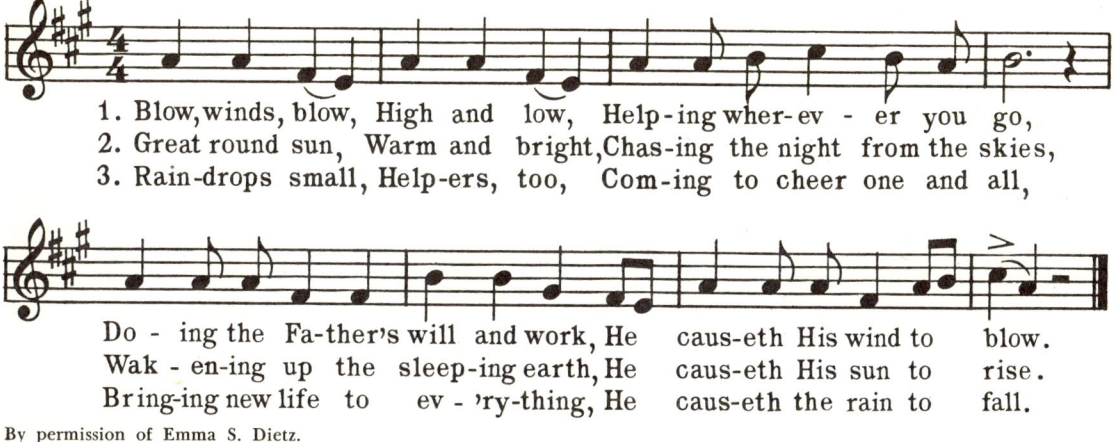

1. Blow, winds, blow, High and low, Help-ing wher-ev-er you go,
2. Great round sun, Warm and bright, Chas-ing the night from the skies,
3. Rain-drops small, Help-ers, too, Com-ing to cheer one and all,

Do-ing the Fa-ther's will and work, He caus-eth His wind to blow.
Wak-en-ing up the sleep-ing earth, He caus-eth His sun to rise.
Bring-ing new life to ev-'ry-thing, He caus-eth the rain to fall.

By permission of Emma S. Dietz.

We Thank Thee

Ralph W. Emerson
Paul Ambrose

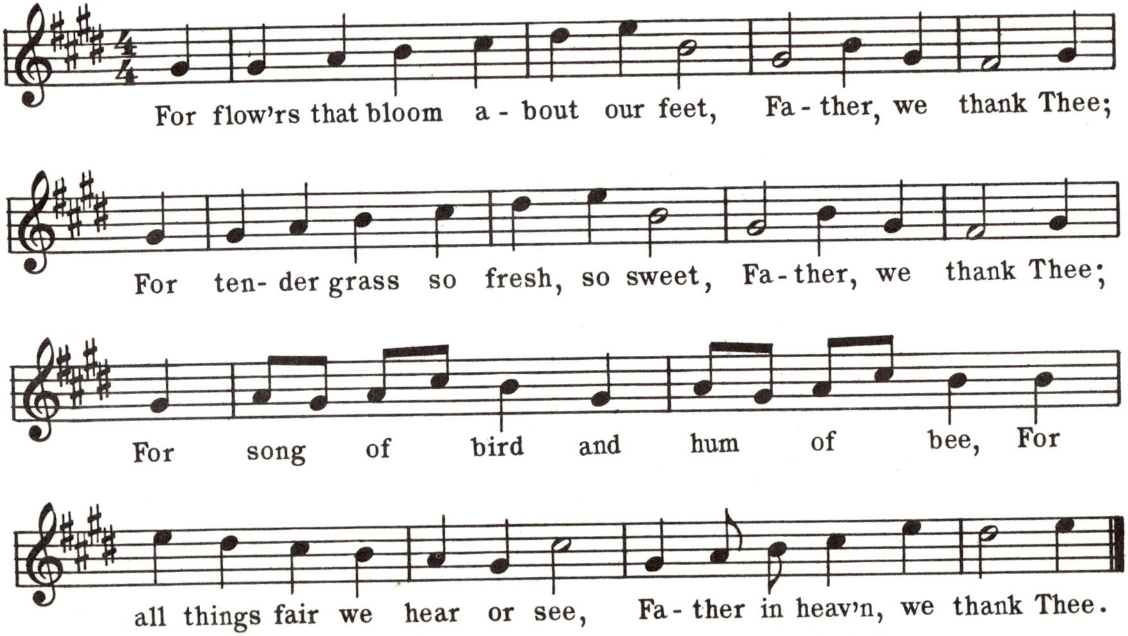

For flow'rs that bloom a-bout our feet, Fa-ther, we thank Thee;

For ten-der grass so fresh, so sweet, Fa-ther, we thank Thee;

For song of bird and hum of bee, For

all things fair we hear or see, Fa-ther in heav'n, we thank Thee.

From *Music Hour*, Book III. Used by special permission of Silver Burdett Company, New York.

A Springtime Prayer

Frances Weld Danielson
Melody from Mozart

We're thank-ful for the spring-time, Lord; For birds and trees and flowers; For sing-ing brooks and hum-ming bees; For sun-ny, hap-py hours.

From *Songs for Little People*, by Danielson and Conant. Copyright, the Pilgrim Press. Used by permission.

'Tis God Who Sends the Spring

Arranged from El Heerwart's Collection
Mendelssohn

1. I'm ver-y glad the spring has come, The sun shines out so bright; The lit-tle birds up-on the trees Are sing-ing with de-light.
2. I love to see the pret-ty flow'rs That rain and sun-shine bring; When all things seem just like my-self So glad to see the spring.
3. God must be ver-y good in-deed, Who made each pret-ty thing; For flow'rs and birds and sun-shine say 'Tis God who sends the spring.

By permission of Emma S. Dietz.

Summertime

Anonymous
Folk Tune

1. I like the cheerful summertime, With all its birds and flow'rs,
2. I like to hear the little birds, That carol on the trees;
3. I like the bright and glorious sun, That gives us light and heat;
4. It lifts my heart to God, who made These pleasant things for me;

Its shining garments green and smooth, Its cool, refreshing show'rs.
I like the gentle murm'ring stream; I like the evening breeze.
I like the pearly drops of dew That sparkle 'neath my feet.
Who gave me life, and health, and strength, And eyes that I might see.

Autumn

Ida F. Leyda
Helen M. Browne

1. Apples mellow, Pumpkins yellow, Tell the time of year;
2. Colors gaily Changing daily, Brighten field and wood;

Nuts are falling, Nature calling, Autumn time is here.
Autumn's glory Tells the story, God is great and good.

By permission of Emma S. Dietz.

Praise to God, Immortal Praise

Anna L. Barbauld · Asahel Abbot

1. Praise to God, im-mor-tal praise, For the love that crowns our days;
2. For the bless-ings of the field, For the stores the gar-dens yield,
3. Clouds that drop re-fresh-ing dews; Suns that ge-nial heat dif-fuse;
4. All that Spring with boun-teous hand, Scat-ters o'er the smil-ing land;
5. These, great God, to Thee we owe, Source whence all our bless-ings flow;

Boun-teous source of ev-'ry joy, Let Thy praise our tongues em-ploy.
For the joy which har-vests bring, Grate-ful prais-es now we sing.
Flocks that whit-en all the plain, Yel-low sheaves of rip-ened grain.
All that lib-'ral Au-tumn pours From her o-ver-flow-ing stores;
And for these our souls shall raise Grate-ful vows and sol-emn praise.

Winter Song

Nancy Byrd Turner — Somerset Folk Song

1. A-bove the world the win-ter stars, The love-ly stars, look down
On snow-y wood and si-lent hill, On road and field and town—
So clear and far, so calm and bright, God's glo-ry in the night.

2. A-cross the dark the win-ter dawn Comes slow-ly up the sky,
Fair col-ors spread-ing north and south, Like ban-ners lift-ed high.
O rose and gold and red un-furled A-bove God's love-ly world!

Words used by permission of Nancy Byrd Turner.

Another Year Is Dawning

Frances Ridley Havergal — Melchior Vulpius

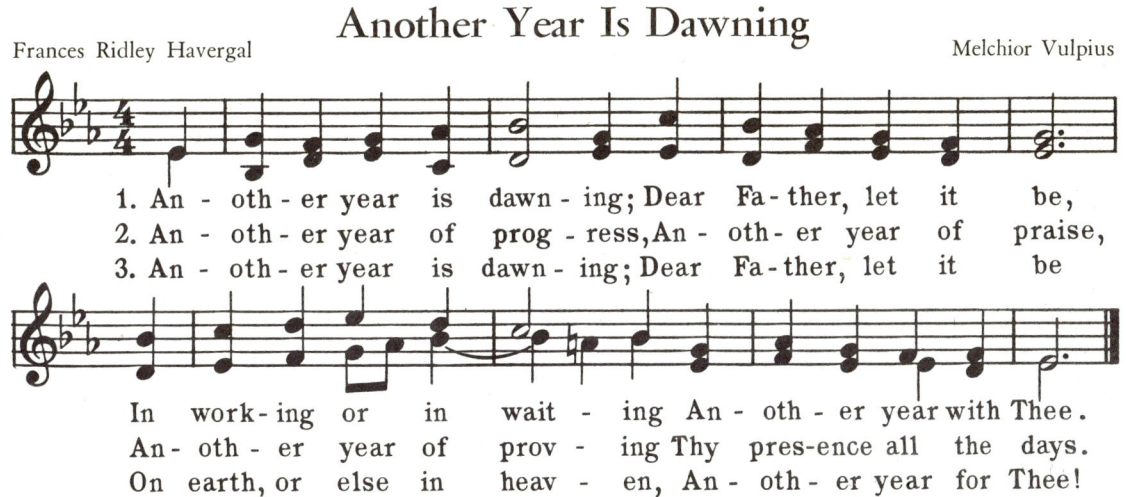

1. An-oth-er year is dawn-ing; Dear Fa-ther, let it be,
In work-ing or in wait-ing An-oth-er year with Thee.

2. An-oth-er year of prog-ress, An-oth-er year of praise,
An-oth-er year of prov-ing Thy pres-ence all the days.

3. An-oth-er year is dawn-ing; Dear Fa-ther, let it be
On earth, or else in heav-en, An-oth-er year for Thee!

From *New Music Horizons*, Book III. Used by special permission of Silver Burdett Company, New York.

Father, We Bring Thee Our Praises

From *Music Hour* Book II. Used by special permission of Silver Burdett Company, New York.

God Loves Me

From *Father, Hear Thy Children Sing*, copyright 1953, by Hall & McCreary Company. Used by permission.

God Sees the Little Sparrow Fall

Maria Straub
S. W. Straub

1. God sees the lit-tle spar-row fall, It meets His ten-der view;
2. He paints the lil-y of the field, Per-fumes each lil-y bell;
3. God made the lit-tle birds and flow'rs, And all things large and small;

If God so loves the lit-tle birds, I know He loves me, too.
If He so loves the lit-tle flow'rs, I know He loves me well.
He'll not for-get His lit-tle ones, I know He loves them all.

REFRAIN

He loves me, too, He loves me, too, I know He loves me, too;

Be-cause He loves the lit-tle things, I know He loves me, too.

Copyright, by David C. Cook Publishing Co. Used by permission.

37

Praise and Thanks

Anna G. Whitmore
Netherlands Tune

We pray to our Father When night is de-scend-ing;
When morn-ing is break-ing We sing to His praise.
With wis-dom and love And kind-ness nev-er end-ing
He guards us and pro-tects us And guides all our ways.

From *New Music Horizons*, Book III. Used by special permission of Silver Burdett Company, New York.

Sing to God in Joyful Voice

Virginia C. Murdock
Spanish Hymn

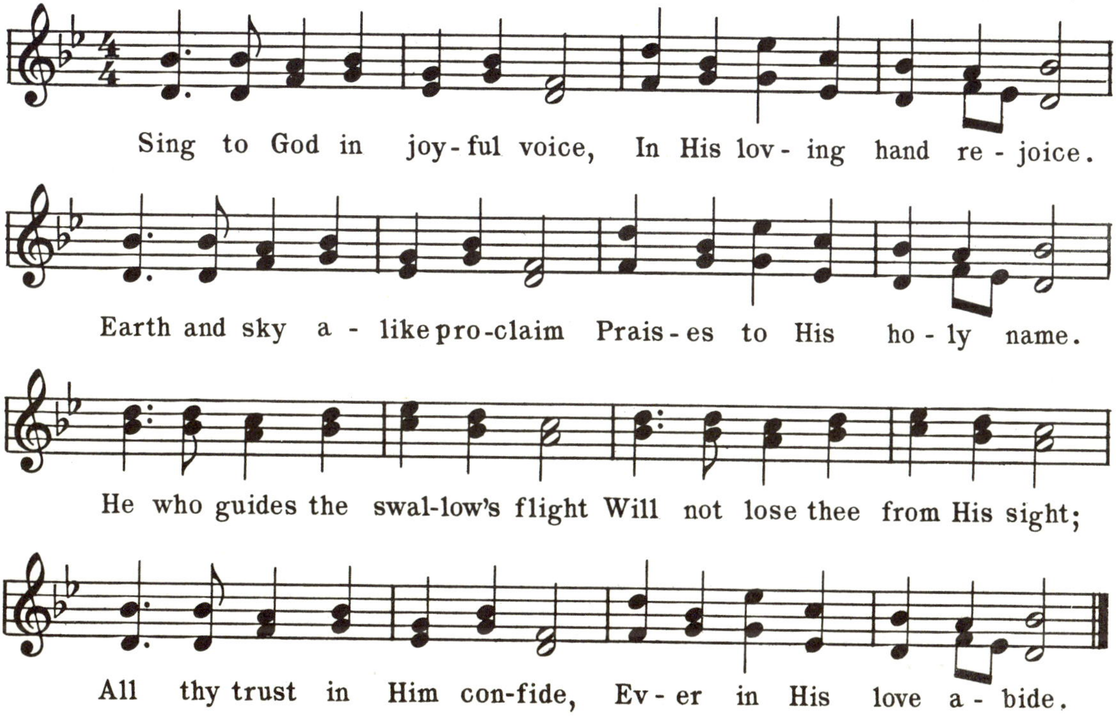

Sing to God in joy-ful voice, In His lov-ing hand re-joice.

Earth and sky a-like pro-claim Prais-es to His ho-ly name.

He who guides the swal-low's flight Will not lose thee from His sight;

All thy trust in Him con-fide, Ev-er in His love a-bide.

From *New Music Horizons*, Book III. Used by special permission of Silver Burdett Company, New York.

Great Things

Psalm 126:3
Jean Kremer

The Lord hath done great things for us, Where-of we are glad.

Used by permission.

39

Faithful Is God

Translated from the German by A. C. Stellhorn
Old German Melody

1. Faith-ful is God, Faith-ful is God! His Word is sure,
2. Faith-ful is God, Faith-ful is God! He tends to us
3. Faith-ful is God, Faith-ful is God! When yet I pray,
4. Faith-ful is God, Faith-ful is God! Thus praise in good

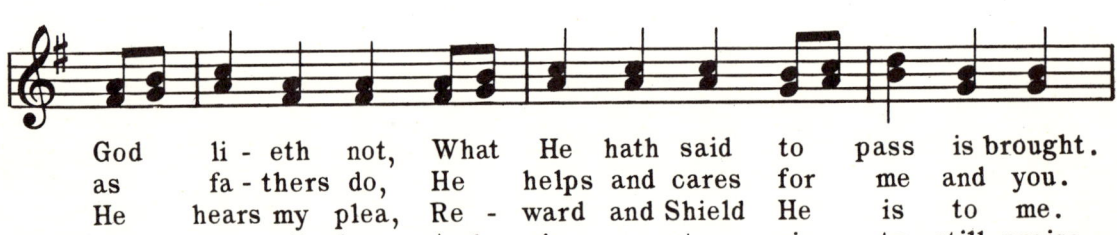

God li-eth not, What He hath said to pass is brought.
as fa-thers do, He helps and cares for me and you.
He hears my plea, Re-ward and Shield He is to me.
and e-vil days, And in e-ter-ni-ty still praise,

Yes, He keeps faith; yes, He keeps faith.
Yes, He keeps faith; yes, He keeps faith.
Yes, He keeps faith; yes, He keeps faith.
For He keeps faith; for He keeps faith.

From MUSIC READER *for Lutheran Schools*. Used by permission of Concordia Publishing House.

Thou Art with Us

Florence M. Taylor
Dimitri Bortniansky

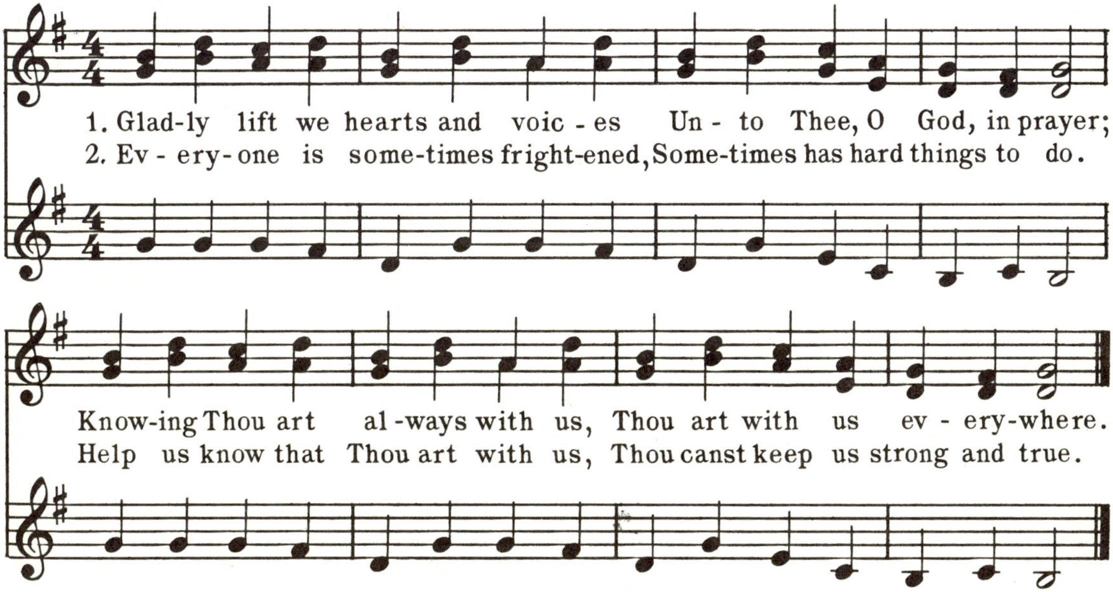

1. Glad-ly lift we hearts and voic-es Un-to Thee, O God, in prayer;
2. Ev-ery-one is some-times fright-ened, Some-times has hard things to do.

Know-ing Thou art al-ways with us, Thou art with us ev-ery-where.
Help us know that Thou art with us, Thou canst keep us strong and true.

From *Children's Religion*, copyright, the Pilgrim Press. Used by permission.

Thanking God

Martha Wonn
Martha Wonn

Thank Him for work and play, Thank Him for night and day,

Thank Him for songs we sing, Thank Him for ev-'ry-thing.

From *The American Singer*, Book I, by Beattie and Wolverton. Used by permission of American Book Company.

Thy Mercies, Lord
Canon   Tallis

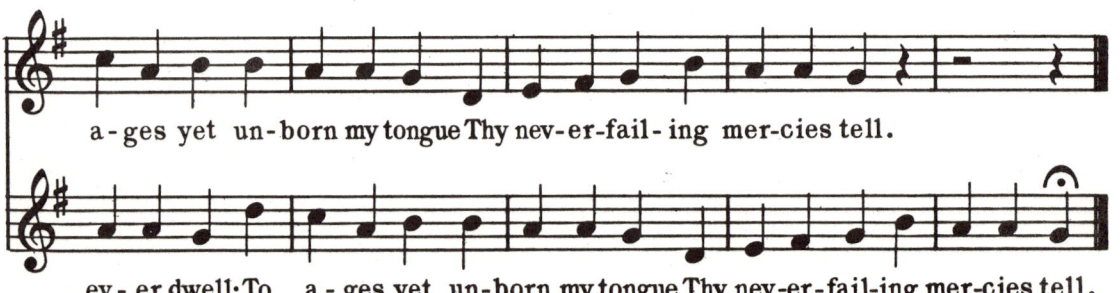

From *New Elementary Music*, by Charles A. Fullerton.

Praise Him

Clara Belle Baker

Fa-ther and moth-er who give us lov-ing care,

Praise Him, praise Him, praise Him our God. Sing, lit-tle chil-dren, oh! sing ev-ery-where.

From *Songs for the Little Child* by Baker and Kohlsaat. Copyright renewal 1949 by Clara Belle Baker. By permission of Abingdon Press.

Praise to God for Things We See

Matilda M. Penstone   Arranged from a French Folk Song by Roberta Bitgood

1. Praise to God for things we see, Grow-ing flower and wav-ing tree,
2. Praise to God for things we hear, Voic-es of our play-mates dear,

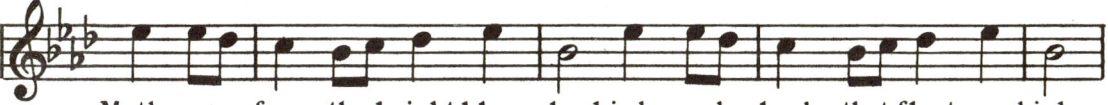

Moth-er's face, the bright blue sky, birds and clouds that float on high,
Mer-ry bells, the songs of birds, Sto-ries, tunes, and kind-ly words,

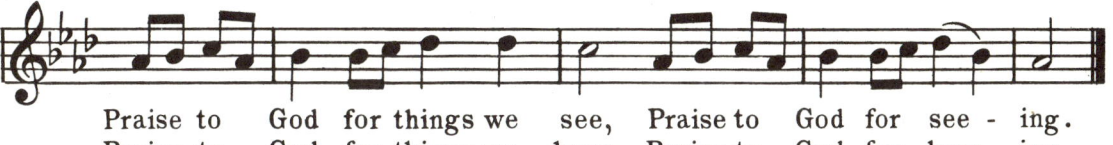

Praise to God for things we see, Praise to God for see-ing.
Praise to God for things we hear, Praise to God for hear-ing.

Words and music from *Hymns for Primary Worship*, copyright 1946 by the Westminster Press. Used by permission.

Can a Little Child Like Me?

Mary Mapes Dodge W. K. Bassford

1. Can a lit-tle child like me Thank the Fa-ther fit-ting-ly?
2. For the fruit up-on the tree, For the birds that sing of Thee;
3. For our com-rades and our plays, And our hap-py hol-i-days;

Yes, oh yes, be good and true, Pa-tient, kind, in all you do;
For the earth in beau-ty dressed, Fa-ther, moth-er, and the rest;
For the joy-ful work and true That a lit-tle child may do;

Love the Lord and do your part, Learn to say with all your heart,
For Thy pre-cious, lov-ing care, For Thy boun-ty ev-'ry-where,
For our lives but just be-gun, For the great gift of Thy Son,

Refrain

Fa-ther, we thank Thee, Fa-ther, we thank Thee, Fa-ther in heav-en, we thank Thee!
Fa-ther, we thank Thee, Fa-ther, we thank Thee, Fa-ther in heav-en, we thank Thee!
Fa-ther, we thank Thee, Fa-ther, we thank Thee, Fa-ther in heav-en, we thank Thee!

Words from *St. Nicholas Magazine.* Used by permission of Appleton-Century-Crofts, Inc.

We Thank Thee, Father, for Our Homes

Elizabeth McE. Shields　　　　　　　　　　　　　　　　　　Miriam Drury

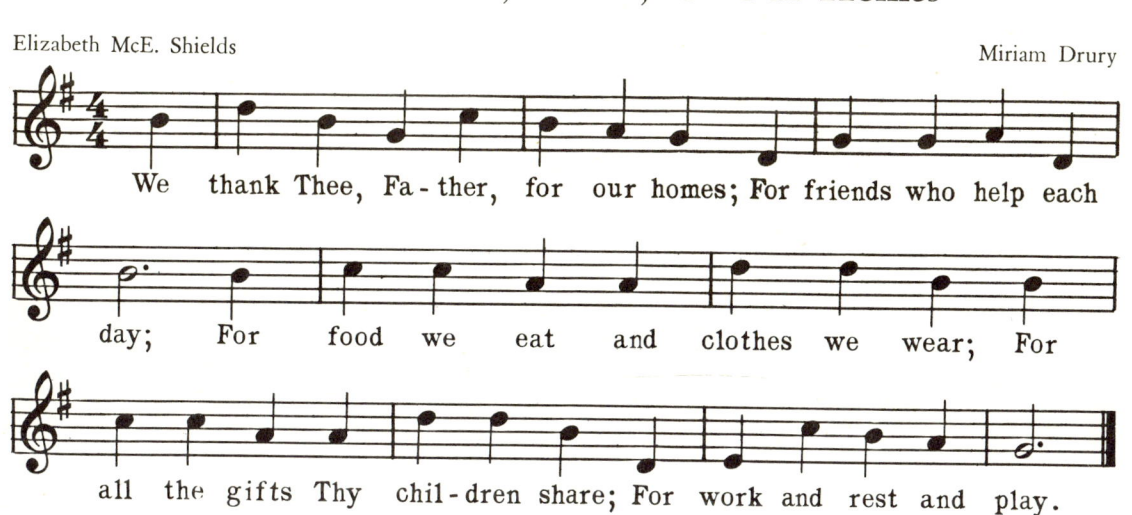

We thank Thee, Father, for our homes; For friends who help each day; For food we eat and clothes we wear; For all the gifts Thy chil-dren share; For work and rest and play.

Words from *The Westminster Leader*, copyright, 1928, by the Presbyterian Board of Christian Education.
Music from *When the Little Child Wants to Sing*, copyright, 1935, by the Presbyterian Board of Christian Education.

We Thank Thee, Loving Father

H. German

We thank Thee, lov-ing Fa-ther, For all Thy ten-der care,
For food and clothes and shel-ter And all Thy world so fair.

Adapted from *Songs for the Little Child* by Baker and Kohlsaat. Copyright renewal 1949 by Clara Bell Baker. By permission of Abingdon Press.

A Child's Prayer

I

Elizabeth McE. Shields   W. Lawrence Curry

We thank Thee, lov-ing Fa-ther, For sleep and food and play; For watch-ing through the night-time, And help-ing us by day.

Words from *Beginners Story Leaflets*, copyright, 1930, by the Presbyterian Board of Christian Education. Music copyright, 1935, from *When the Little Child Wants to Sing*.

Lord, I Would Own Thy Tender Care

Jane Taylor John Day

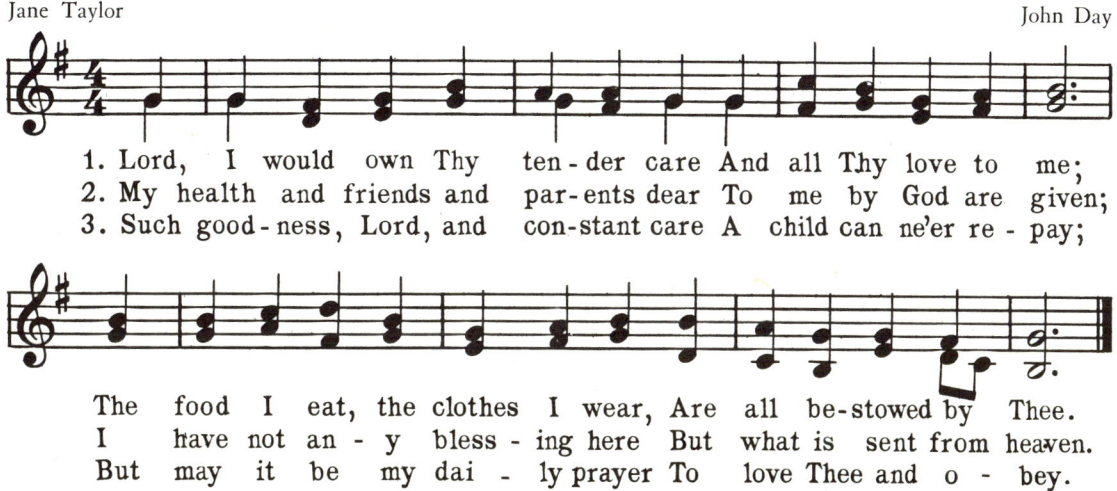

1. Lord, I would own Thy tender care And all Thy love to me;
   The food I eat, the clothes I wear, Are all bestowed by Thee.
2. My health and friends and parents dear To me by God are given;
   I have not any blessing here But what is sent from heaven.
3. Such goodness, Lord, and constant care A child can ne'er repay;
   But may it be my daily prayer To love Thee and obey.

We Give Thanks

Adapted from Franz Schubert

We give thanks to Thee, O God. We give thanks to Thee, O God.

Adapted from *Sing, Children, Sing*, copyright 1939 by Edith Lovell Thomas. By permission of Abingdon Press.

Father, Hear Thy Children Sing

Florence O'Keane Whelan F.O.W.

1. Fa-ther, hear Thy chil-dren sing Our songs of love and praise Toward Thee, who art all good and true, Our grate-ful hearts we raise.
2. We know that You love us all, And lis-ten when we pray. Please keep us in Your lov-ing care And bless us ev-'ry day.

From *Father, Hear Thy Children Sing*, copyright 1953, by Hall & McCreary Company. Used by permission.

The Prayer of the Children

Carey Bonner C.B.

1. Lord of all things bright and fair, God, whose love is ev-'ry-where, Thou dost for the chil-dren care; Hear us, heav'n-ly Fa-ther.
2. Wilt Thou al-ways near us stay, When we sleep, or work, or play, Guard and lead us ev-'ry day? Hear us, heav'n-ly Fa-ther.
3. Make us "chil-dren of the light," Help us try to do the right, Serv-ing Thee with all our might; Hear us, heav'n-ly Fa-ther.

Words and music copyright, 1908, by The National Sunday School Union.

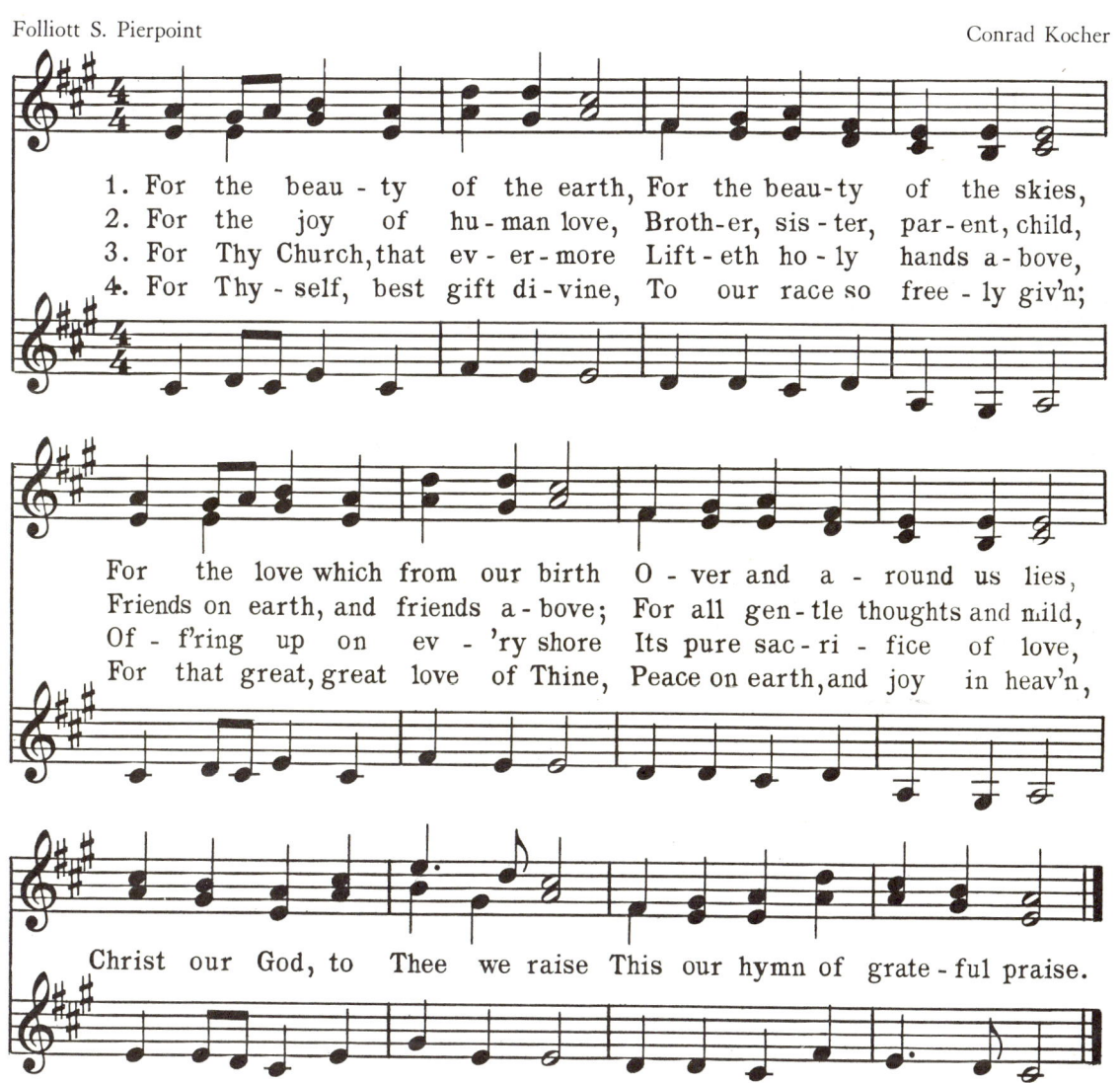

Prayer for Peace

Isabel Innes · Welsh Hymn Tune

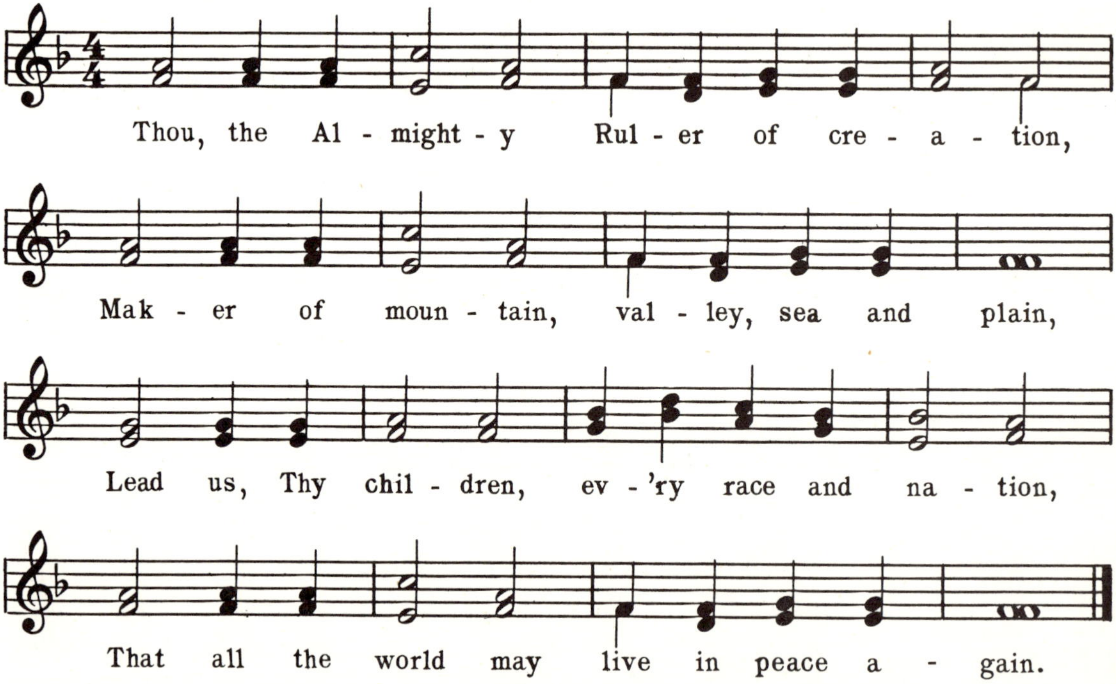

Thou, the Al - might - y Rul - er of cre - a - tion,
Mak - er of moun - tain, val - ley, sea and plain,
Lead us, Thy chil - dren, ev - 'ry race and na - tion,
That all the world may live in peace a - gain.

From *The American Singer*, Book IV, by Beattie and Wolverton. Used by permission of American Book Company.

Hear Our Prayer, O Lord

George Whelpton

Hear our pray'r, O Lord, Hear our pray'r, O Lord,

In-cline Thine ear to us, And grant us Thy peace.

Father, Teach Me

Jane E. Leeson Carl Maria von Weber

Fa-ther, teach me day by day Thy sweet les-son to o-bey;

Sweet-er les-son can-not be, Lov-ing Thee who first loved me.

Father, Lead Me Day by Day

John P. Hopps
George C. Strattner

Fa-ther, lead me day by day, Ev-er in Thine own strong way;
Teach me to be pure and true, Show me what I ought to do.

Lord, Teach a Little Child to Pray

Jane Taylor
William B. Bradbury

1. Lord, teach a lit-tle child to pray, And then, ac-cept my prayer!
2. A lit-tle spar-row can-not fall, Un-no-ticed, Lord, by Thee;
3. Teach me to do what-e'er is right, And when I sin, for-give,

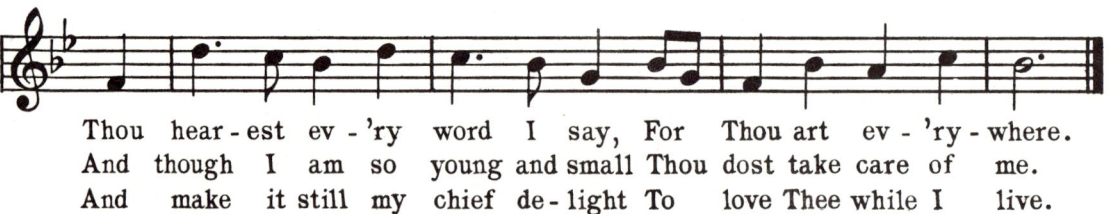

Thou hear-est ev-'ry word I say, For Thou art ev-'ry-where.
And though I am so young and small Thou dost take care of me.
And make it still my chief de-light To love Thee while I live.

A Child's Prayer

The Modern Music Series   II   Carl Reinecke

1. Heav'n-ly Fa-ther, lov-ing, ten-der, Thanks to Thee Thy chil-dren ren-der;
2. In our work-ing, in our play-ing, When our pray'rs to Thee we're say-ing,

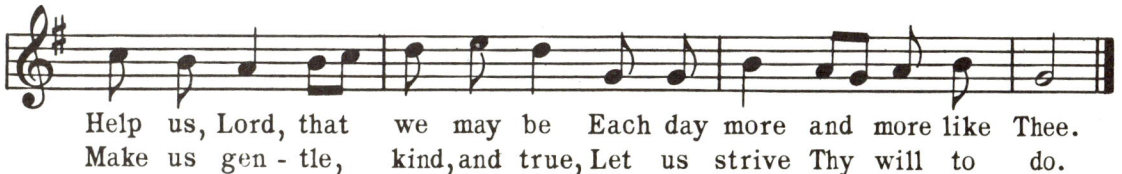

Help us, Lord, that we may be Each day more and more like Thee.
Make us gen-tle, kind, and true, Let us strive Thy will to do.

From *Music Hour*, Book IV. Used by special permission of Silver Burdett Company, New York.

Thank You, God, for All I Have

John Oxenham   John Stainer

1. Thank You, God, for all I have, Keep and bless all those I love,
2. Help me, God, at school to-day, Help me in my work and play,

Help me al-ways, God, to do Just as You would wish me to.
Help me to be brave and true, Help me, Lord, in all I do!

Words from *First Prayers for Children*, by John Oxenham and Roderic Dunkerley. Used by permission.

Teach Us to Pray

Gregorian Chant

1. O God, whose love enfolds us all,
Whose bounty only waits our call,
Teach us, your children, how to pray,
To seek your guidance day by day.

2. O God, whose help is ever near,
Teach us the love that knows no fear,
That, trusting in your holy might,
We live the truth and love the right.

From *New Elementary Music*, by Charles A. Fullerton.

The First Christmas Night

Julie Gibault Carl Wilhelm

1. Ba - by Jesus was born in Beth-le-hem
2. Flocks were graz-ing and shep-herds lis-ten-ing
3. "Come to Beth-le-hem, come to Beth-le-hem,"

Long a - go on a win - ter night;
There on Beth-le-hem's qui - et hill;
An - gels sang in the star - ry light;

In the calm still-ness stars in the heav-ens
An - gels from heav - en came to them sing-ing,
"Wor-ship the Christ Child, sing al - le - lu - ia,

Bathed the vil - lage and sta - ble in light.
Sing - ing car - ols and songs of good will.
Come to Beth - le - hem's sta - ble to - night."

From *The American Singer*, Book II, by Beattie and Wolverton.
Used by permission of American Book Company

Bethlehem

Author Unknown
Grace V. Wilson

1. Winds through the ol-ive trees Soft-ly did blow,
2. Then from the hap-py sky, An-gels bent low,

Round lit-tle Beth-le-hem, Long, long a-go.
Sing-ing their songs of joy, Long, long a-go.

Sheep on the hill-side lay Whit-er than snow;
For in a man-ger bed, Cra-dled we know,

Shep-herds were watch-ing them, Long, long a-go.
Christ came to Beth-le-hem, Long, long a-go.

From *New Music Horizons*, Book II. Used by special permission of Silver Burdett Company, New York.

O Little Town of Bethlehem

Phillips Brooks L. H. Redner

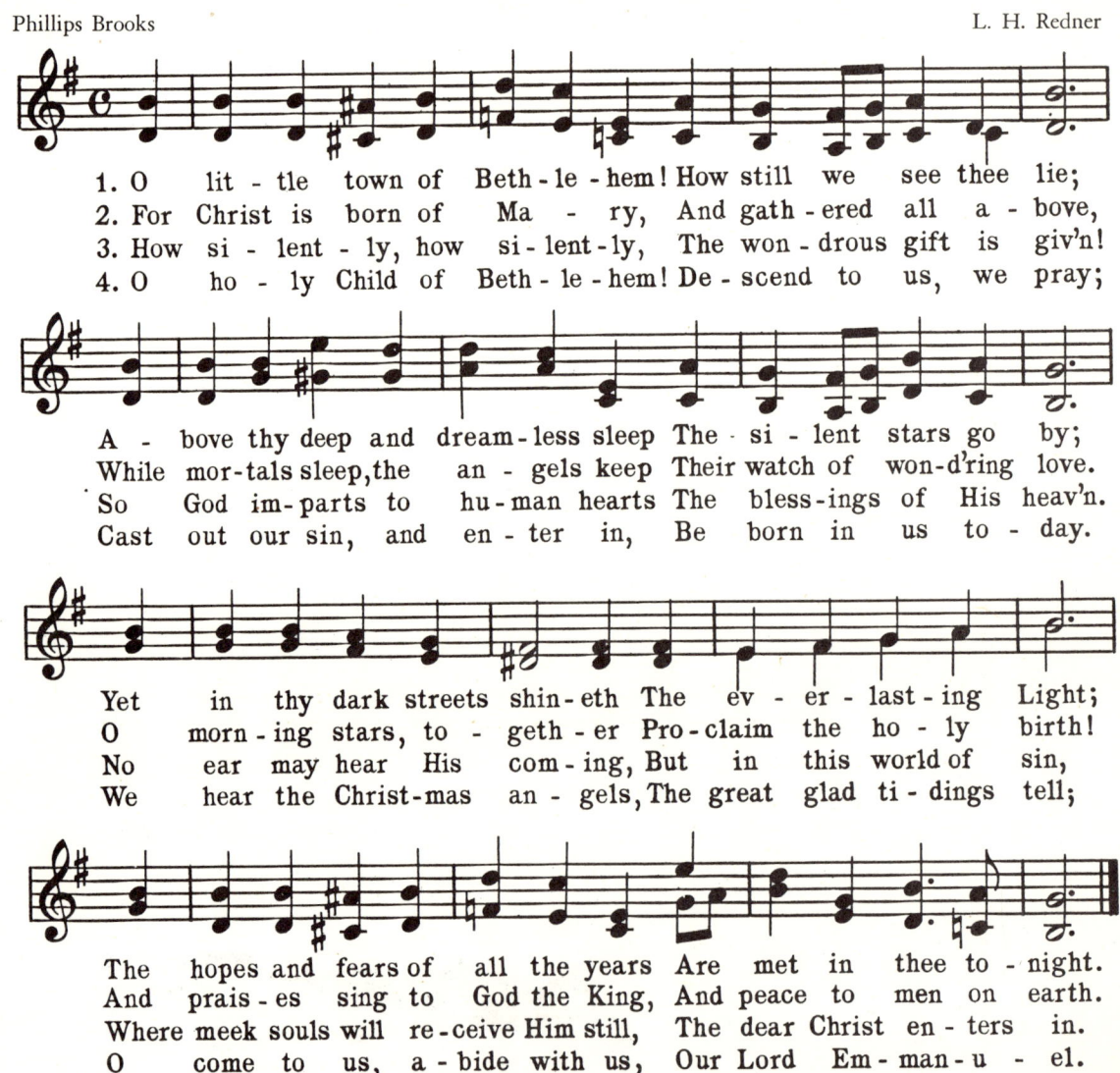

1. O little town of Bethlehem! How still we see thee lie;
Above thy deep and dreamless sleep The silent stars go by;
Yet in thy dark streets shineth The everlasting Light;
The hopes and fears of all the years Are met in thee tonight.

2. For Christ is born of Mary, And gathered all above,
While mortals sleep, the angels keep Their watch of wond'ring love.
O morning stars, together Proclaim the holy birth!
And praises sing to God the King, And peace to men on earth.

3. How silently, how silently, The wondrous gift is giv'n!
So God imparts to human hearts The blessings of His heav'n.
No ear may hear His coming, But in this world of sin,
Where meek souls will receive Him still, The dear Christ enters in.

4. O holy Child of Bethlehem! Descend to us, we pray;
Cast out our sin, and enter in, Be born in us today.
We hear the Christmas angels, The great glad tidings tell;
O come to us, abide with us, Our Lord Emmanuel.

58

Welcome, Holy Night

Translated from German by Anna Hoppe   Old German Tune

1. Wel - come, thou ho - ly, won - der - ful night,
2. Beth - le - hem's plains were slum - b'ring in night,
3. "To you is born Christ Je - sus, the Lord,"

Com - ing to bring us joy and de - light.
When sud - den glo - ry filled them with light.
Thus sang the an - gels with one ac - cord.

An - thems of young and old sweet - ly blend,
An - gels praised God in beau - ti - ful strain,
"Glo - ry to God," O glo - rious re - frain,

Car - ols of joy to heav - en as - cend.
Sing - ing of peace and good will to men.
Ring out with might and cheer us a - gain!

From MUSIC READER *for Lutheran Schools.* Used by permission of Concordia Publishing House.

Silent Night

Joseph Mohr · Franz Gruber

1. Silent night! Holy night! All is calm, all is bright,
2. Silent night! Holy night! Shepherds quake at the sight!
3. Silent night! Holy night! Son of God, love's pure light

Round yon virgin mother and Child; Holy Infant, so tender and mild,
Glories stream from heaven afar, Heav'nly hosts sing alleluia.
Radiant beams from Thy holy face, With the dawn of redeeming grace,

Sleep in heavenly peace, Sleep in heavenly peace.
Christ, the Saviour, is born! Christ, the Saviour, is born.
Jesus, Lord, at Thy birth, Jesus, Lord, at Thy birth.

Baby Jesus

Elizabeth McE. Shields W. Lawrence Curry

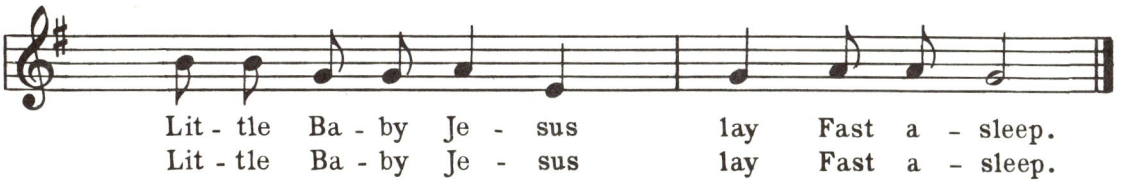

1. On a bed of sweet, new hay, In a sta-ble far a-way,
2. And His moth-er, al-ways near, Cud-dled up the Ba-by dear.

Lit-tle Ba-by Je-sus lay Fast a-sleep.
Lit-tle Ba-by Je-sus lay Fast a-sleep.

From *When the Little Child Wants to Sing*, copyright, 1935, by the Presbyterian Board of Christian Education.

Little Baby Jesus

Ethel L. Smithers Natalia Robinson

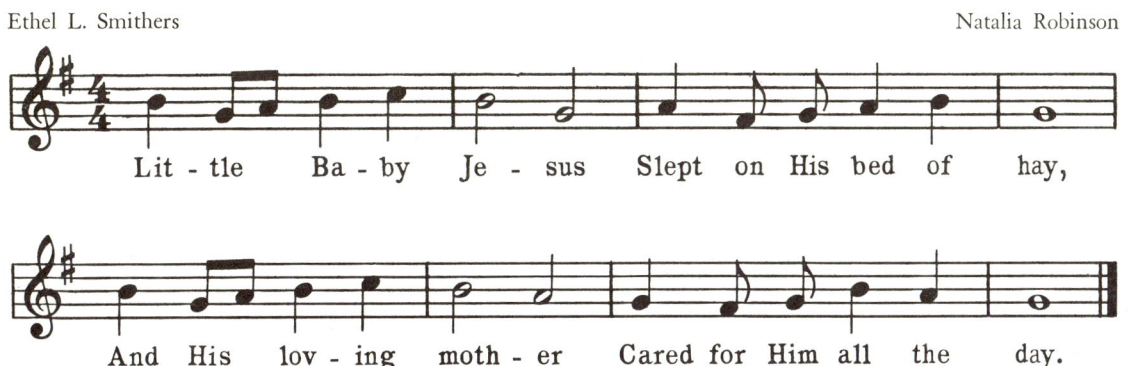

Lit-tle Ba-by Je-sus Slept on His bed of hay,
And His lov-ing moth-er Cared for Him all the day.

Copyright, 1931, by Ethel L. Smithers. Used by permission.

And shep-herds are kneel-ing De-vout-ly in prayer.
O sing till your voic-es Re-ech-o their praise.
O give Him de-vo-tion: O give Him your heart.

Christmas Chorale

Translated by John Troutbeck and Catherine Winkworth   Johann Sebastian Bach

1. With-in yon low-ly man-ger lies The Lord who reigns a-bove the skies;
2. Good news from heav'n the an-gels bring, Glad ti-dings to the earth they sing.

With-in the stall where beasts have fed The Vir-gin-born doth lay His head.
To us this day a Child is giv'n, To crown us with the joy of heav'n.

From *New Music Horizons*, Book IV. Used by special permission of Silver Burdett Company, New York.

Cradled upon a Bed of Hay

C. M.   Walloon Carol

Cra - dled up - on a bed of hay, The lit - tle Babe of

Beth - lehem in a man - ger lay; While shep-herds watch-ing near Heard

an - gel voic - es, clear Sing "Peace on earth! For Christ, the Lord, is born to - day."

Mary's Lullaby

Florence Martin   Arranged by F.M.

Go to sleep, O Child of mine, Lit - tle Je - sus, Babe Di - vine,

You were born in man - ger low - ly But You are the Son of God, most ho - ly.

From *Father, Hear Thy Children Sing*, copyright 1953, by Hall & McCreary Company. Used by permission.

Lullaby to the Christ Child

Arousiag Donigian
Armenian Folk Melody

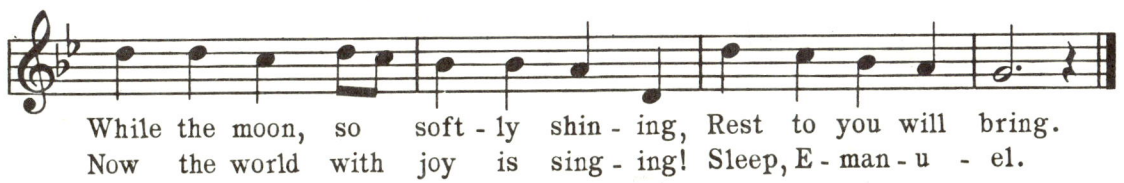

1. Sleep, my ba-by, my be-lov-ed, Lul-la-by I sing, While the moon, so soft-ly shin-ing, Rest to you will bring.
2. Sleep, my ba-by, Ho-ly In-fant, Hope of Is-ra-el; Now the world with joy is sing-ing! Sleep, E-man-u-el.

From *The Whole World Singing*, by Edith Lovell Thomas. Friendship Press. Used by permission.

Shepherds Leave the Hillside

Anonymous

Shep-herds leave the hill-side And their wool-ly sheep. In a crib they find Him, Je-sus, fast a-sleep!

From *Step a Song*. Copyright, 1928, by the Simcoe Publishing Company. Used by permission.

The Holy Child

Translated · Colombian Villancico

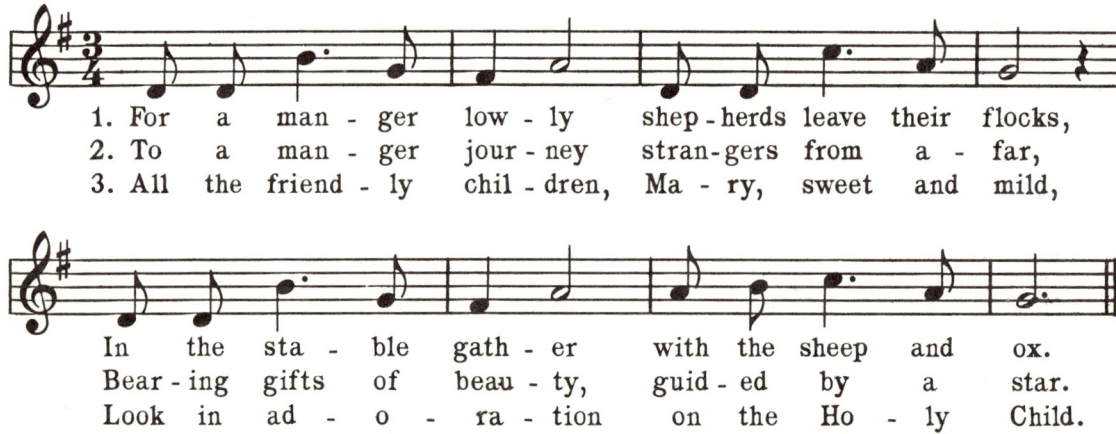

1. For a manger lowly shepherds leave their flocks,
2. To a manger journey strangers from afar,
3. All the friendly children, Mary, sweet and mild,

In the stable gather with the sheep and ox.
Bearing gifts of beauty, guided by a star.
Look in adoration on the Holy Child.

From *The American Singer*, Book IV, by Beattie and Wolverton. Used by permission of American Book Company.

Shepherds, Shake Off Your Drowsy Sleep

From the French · French Carol from Besançon

1. Shepherds, shake off your drowsy sleep, Rise and leave your silly sheep;
2. Hark! even now the bells ring round, Listen to their merry sound;
3. See how the flow'rs all burst anew, Thinking snow is summer dew;

Angels from heav'n around loud singing, Tidings of great joy are bringing.
Hark! how the birds new songs are making, As if winter's chains were breaking.
See how the stars afresh are glowing All their brightest beams bestowing.

CHORUS

Shep-herds! the cho-rus come and swell! Sing No-el, O sing No-el!

From *Music Hour,* Book II. Used by special permission of Silver Burdett Company, New York.

Christmas Carol

Ethel Crowninshield   Austrian Folk Tune

1. Bright star of Christ-mas, The shep-herds have seen you to-night;
2. Low in a man-ger The Beth-le-hem Babe they have found;

Bright star of Christ-mas The wise men will fol-low your light.
Though they be stran-gers, He smiles at them kneel-ing a-round.

O - ver the sta - ble, Where sheep and cat - tle stay,
Gifts they will bring Him, Then up and on their way,

Star, bright - ly shin - ing, You bring the Christ-mas day.
Filled with the won - der Of that first Christ-mas day.

Melody and words from *Rhythms and Rimes* of THE WORLD OF MUSIC, copyright 1936, 1943. Used by permission of Ginn and Company, owner of the copyright.

Carol, Children, Carol

W. A. Muhlenberg
Source Unknown

1. Car-ol, chil-dren, car-ol, Car-ol joy-ful-ly,
2. At the mer-ry ta-ble, Think of those who've none, The

   Car-ol the good ti-dings, Car-ol mer-ri-ly.
   or-phan and the wid-ow, Hun-gry and a-lone.

   And pray a glad-some Christ-mas For all good Chris-tian men.
   Oh, boun-ti-ful the offer-ings You to the al-tar bring;

   Car-ol, chil-dren, car-ol, Christ-mas day a-gain.
   Let the poor and need-y Christ-mas car-ols sing.

REFRAIN

Car-ol, chil-dren, car-ol, Car-ol joy-ful-ly,

Car-ol the good tid-ings, Car-ol mer-ri-ly.

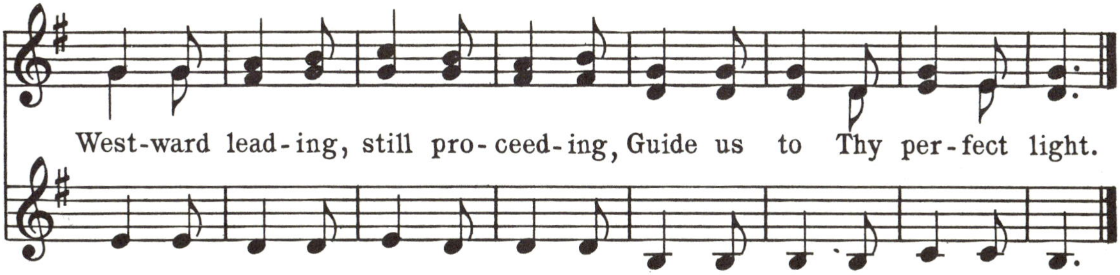

Westward leading, still proceeding, Guide us to Thy perfect light.

From *New Music Horizons*, Book IV. Used by special permission of Silver Burdett Company, New York.

Happy Christmas Day

Marion Bergman
Czech Folk Song

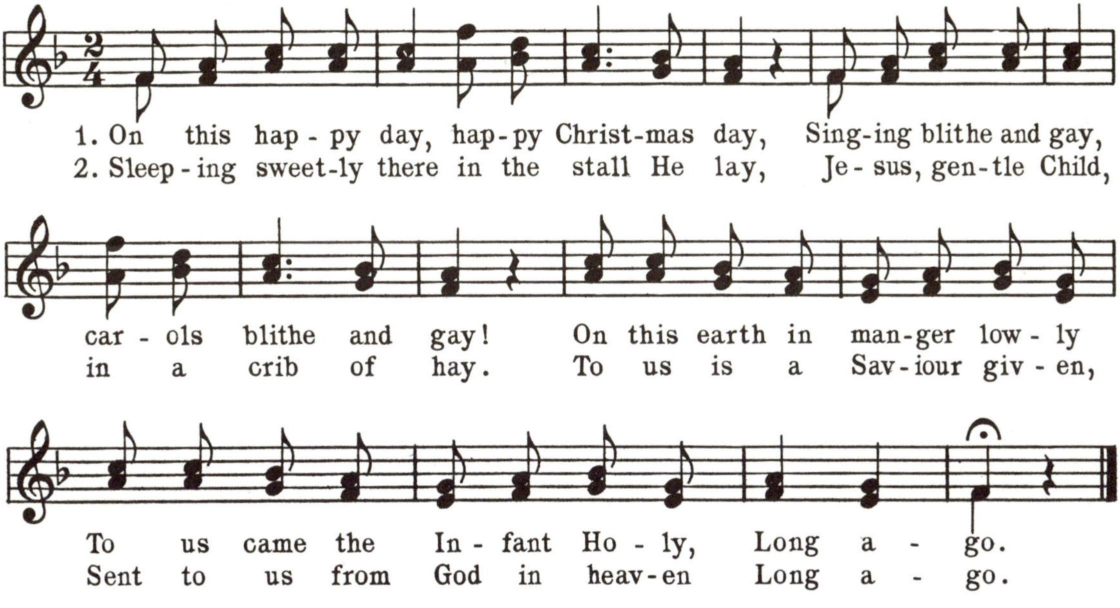

1. On this happy day, happy Christmas day, Singing blithe and gay, carols blithe and gay! On this earth in manger lowly To us came the Infant Holy, Long ago.
2. Sleeping sweetly there in the stall He lay, Jesus, gentle Child, in a crib of hay. To us is a Saviour given, Sent to us from God in heaven Long ago.

From *New Music Horizons*, Book III. Used by special permission of Silver Burdett Company, New York.

Glory to God in the Highest

Adapted from Luke 2:14   Miriam Drury

Glo - ry to God in the high - est! Glo - ry to God in the high - est!

Glo - ry to God in the high - est, For Je - sus is born to - day.

Words and music from *When a Little Child Wants to Sing*, copyright, 1935, by the Presbyterian Board of Christian Education. Used by permission.

Infant So Gentle

From the French   Gascon Carol

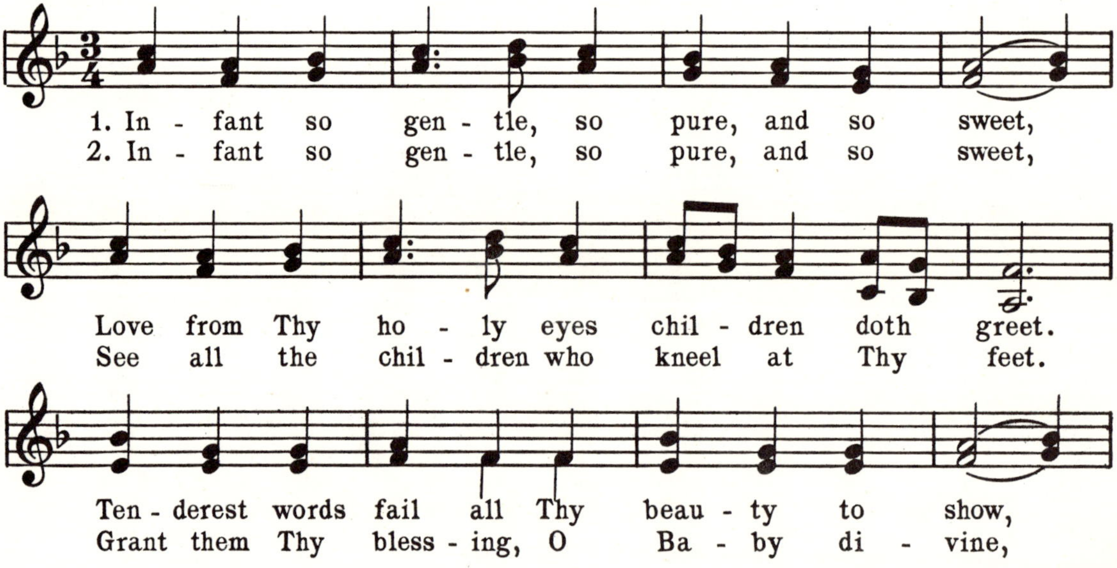

1. In - fant so gen - tle, so pure, and so sweet,
2. In - fant so gen - tle, so pure, and so sweet,

Love from Thy ho - ly eyes chil - dren doth greet.
See all the chil - dren who kneel at Thy feet.

Ten - derest words fail all Thy beau - ty to show,
Grant them Thy bless - ing, O Ba - by di - vine,

76

We must a-dore Thee if Thee we would know.
Lead them un-to Thee and make them all Thine.

From *Hymns for Primary Worship*, Westminster Press.

Joy to the World

Isaac Watts   Arranged from George Frederick Handel by Lowell Mason

1. Joy to the world! the Lord is come! Let earth re-ceive her King;
2. Joy to the earth! the Sav-iour reigns! Let men their songs em-ploy;
3. He rules the world with truth and grace; And makes the na-tions prove

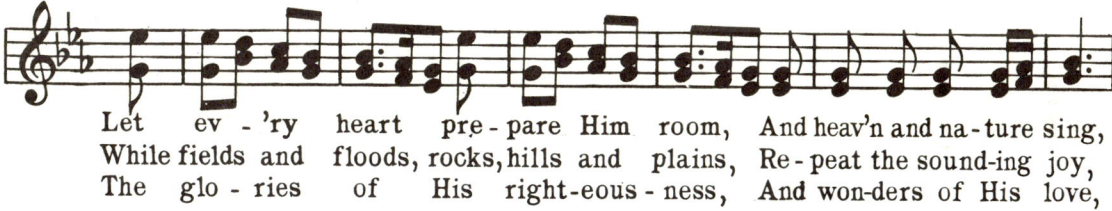

Let ev-'ry heart pre-pare Him room, And heav'n and na-ture sing,
While fields and floods, rocks, hills and plains, Re-peat the sound-ing joy,
The glo-ries of His right-eous-ness, And won-ders of His love,

And heav'n and na-ture sing, And heav'n, and heav'n and na-ture sing.
Re-peat the sound-ing joy; Re-peat, re-peat, the sound-ing joy.
And won-ders of His love, And won-ders, won-ders of His love.

Now Let Your Happy Voices Ring

Adapted from the original by Stephen Fay

Johann Sebastian Bach

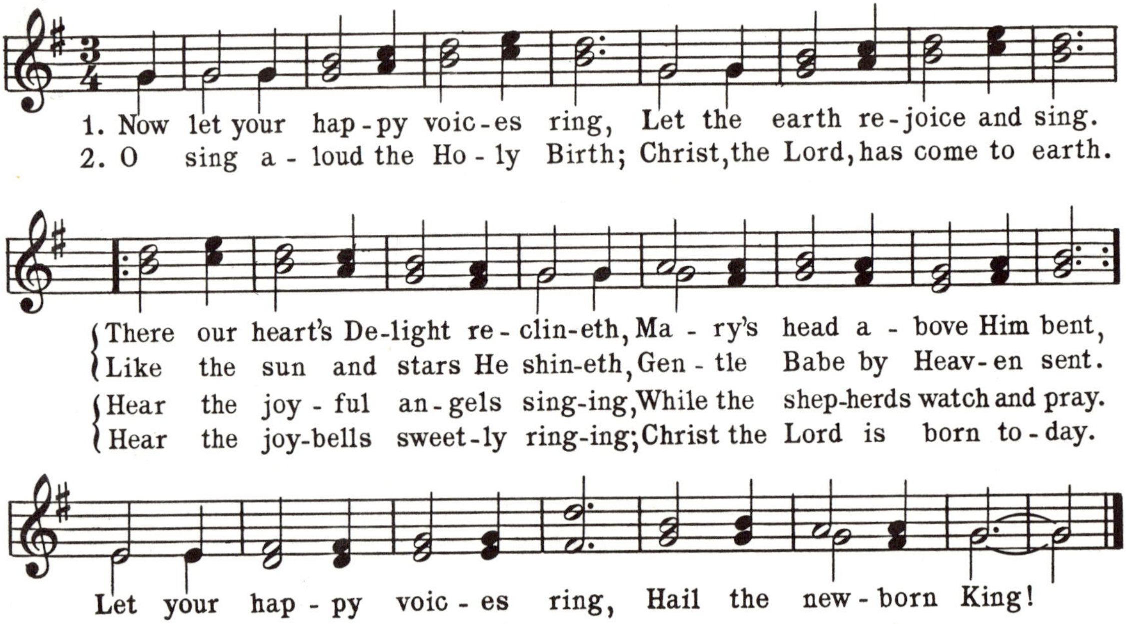

1. Now let your hap-py voic-es ring, Let the earth re-joice and sing.
2. O sing a-loud the Ho-ly Birth; Christ, the Lord, has come to earth.

There our heart's De-light re-clin-eth, Ma-ry's head a-bove Him bent,
Like the sun and stars He shin-eth, Gen-tle Babe by Heav-en sent.
Hear the joy-ful an-gels sing-ing, While the shep-herds watch and pray.
Hear the joy-bells sweet-ly ring-ing; Christ the Lord is born to-day.

Let your hap-py voic-es ring, Hail the new-born King!

From *We Sing*. Used by permission of C. C. Birchard & Company.

Thou Holy Christ-Child, Blest and Dear

E. M. Arndt

G. Siegert

1. Thou ho-ly Christ-child, blest and dear,
2. Thou Christ, to Thee we trib-ute pay
3. Thou ho-ly Christ-child, blest and dear,

78

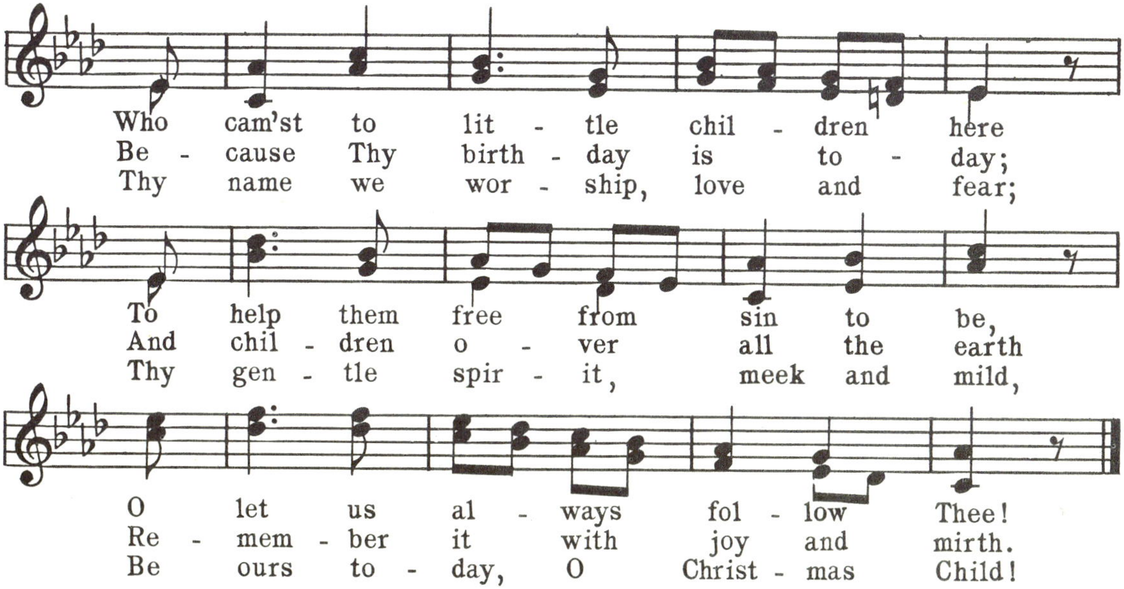

Who cam'st to lit - tle chil - dren here
Be - cause Thy birth - day is to - day;
Thy name we wor - ship, love and fear;

To help them free from sin to be,
And chil - dren o - ver all the earth
Thy gen - tle spir - it, meek and mild,

O let us al - ways fol - low Thee!
Re - mem - ber it with joy and mirth.
Be ours to - day, O Christ - mas Child!

From MUSIC READER for Lutheran Schools. Used by permission of Concordia Publishing House.

When Jesus Was a Little Boy

Grace Noll Crowell
Welsh Tune

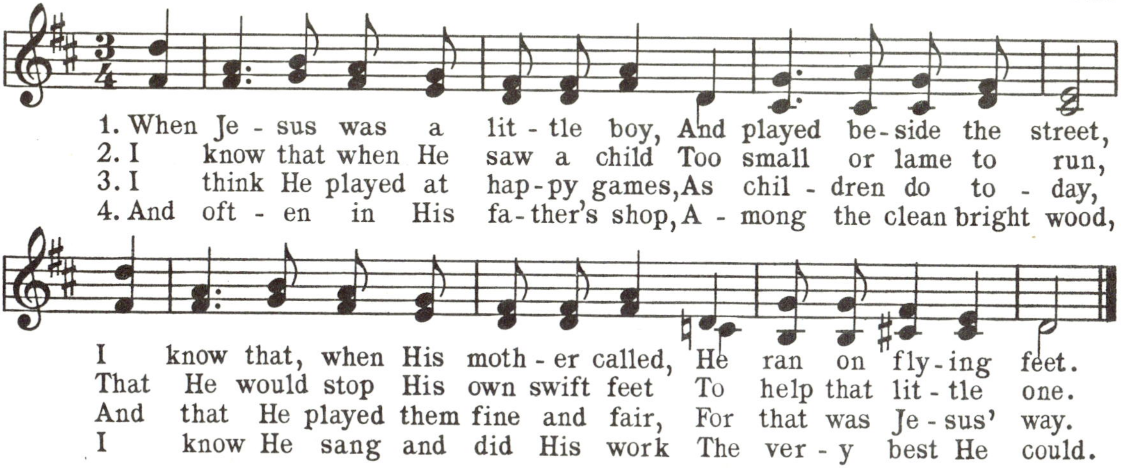

1. When Je - sus was a lit - tle boy, And played be - side the street,
2. I know that when He saw a child Too small or lame to run,
3. I think He played at hap - py games, As chil - dren do to - day,
4. And oft - en in His fa - ther's shop, A - mong the clean bright wood,

I know that, when His moth - er called, He ran on fly - ing feet.
That He would stop His own swift feet To help that lit - tle one.
And that He played them fine and fair, For that was Je - sus' way.
I know He sang and did His work The ver - y best He could.

Used by permission of the author.

In the Temple

Flora Kirkland
Howard E. Smith

1. In the tem-ple, in the tem-ple Stood a lit-tle boy one day, And the doc-tors won-dered great-ly At the words they heard Him say.
2. It was Je-sus who was teach-ing, And they lis-tened to His word, As He told them of His mis-sion From the great and might-y Lord.
3. With the teach-ers there they found Him, Tho' a low-ly, learn-ing youth, But His an-swers as He told them Were com-plete with Bi-ble truth.
4. "Let us ev-er then be loy-al To our God, and church, and home." Ev-er faith-ful, ev-er trust-ing, "Nev-er mind-ing what may come."

CHORUS

It was Je-sus! It was Je-sus! He was but a lit-tle child, But the light of heav'n was shin-ing In His face so pure and mild.

Copyright 1921, Renewal 1949, The Rodeheaver Co., Owner. International Copyright Secured. All rights reserved. Arr. Copyright © 1958 by The Rodeheaver Co. Used by permission.

Jesus Loves Me

Anna B. Warner Wm. B. Bradbury

1. Je-sus loves me! This I know, For the Bi-ble tells me so; Lit-tle
2. Je-sus loves me! He who died Heav-en's gate to o-pen wide! He will
3. Je-sus loves me! Loves me still! Tho' I'm ver-y weak and ill; From His
4. Je-sus loves me! He will stay Close be-side me all the way; If I

ones to Him be-long, They are weak, but He is strong.
wash a-way my sin, Let His lit-tle child come in.
shin-ing home on high, Comes to watch me where I lie. Yes, Je-sus loves me!
love Him, when I die He will take me home on high.

REFRAIN

Yes, Je-sus loves me! Yes, Je-sus loves me! The Bi-ble tells me so.

O, We, the Little Children

Ada Skemp
Ludwig van Beethoven

1. O, we, the little children, Are very glad to know
That Jesus welcomed little ones, And blessed them long ago.
2. We love to hear the stories That Jesus used to tell,
And listen to them o'er and o'er Until we know them well.
3. We want to be His children, And learn to do His will,
And when we're big and quite grown up We want to love Him still.
4. Dear Jesus, bless us children, And help us to be good,
And try to do our duty, As all Thy children should.

Words copyright, 1908, by The Sunday School Union.

Jesus Is the Friend of Children

D. P. Gurley
Chas. Edw. Pollock

1. Jesus is the friend of children, Jesus is the friend of children,
Jesus is the friend of children, We praise Him for His love.
2. He will lead us home to glory, He will lead us home to glory,
He will lead us home to glory, His own bright home above.
3. Jesus is our faithful teacher, Jesus is our faithful teacher,
Jesus is our faithful teacher, We praise Him for His Word.

By permission David C. Cook Publishing Co.

That Sweet Story of Old

Mrs. Jemima Luke · J. C. Englebrecht

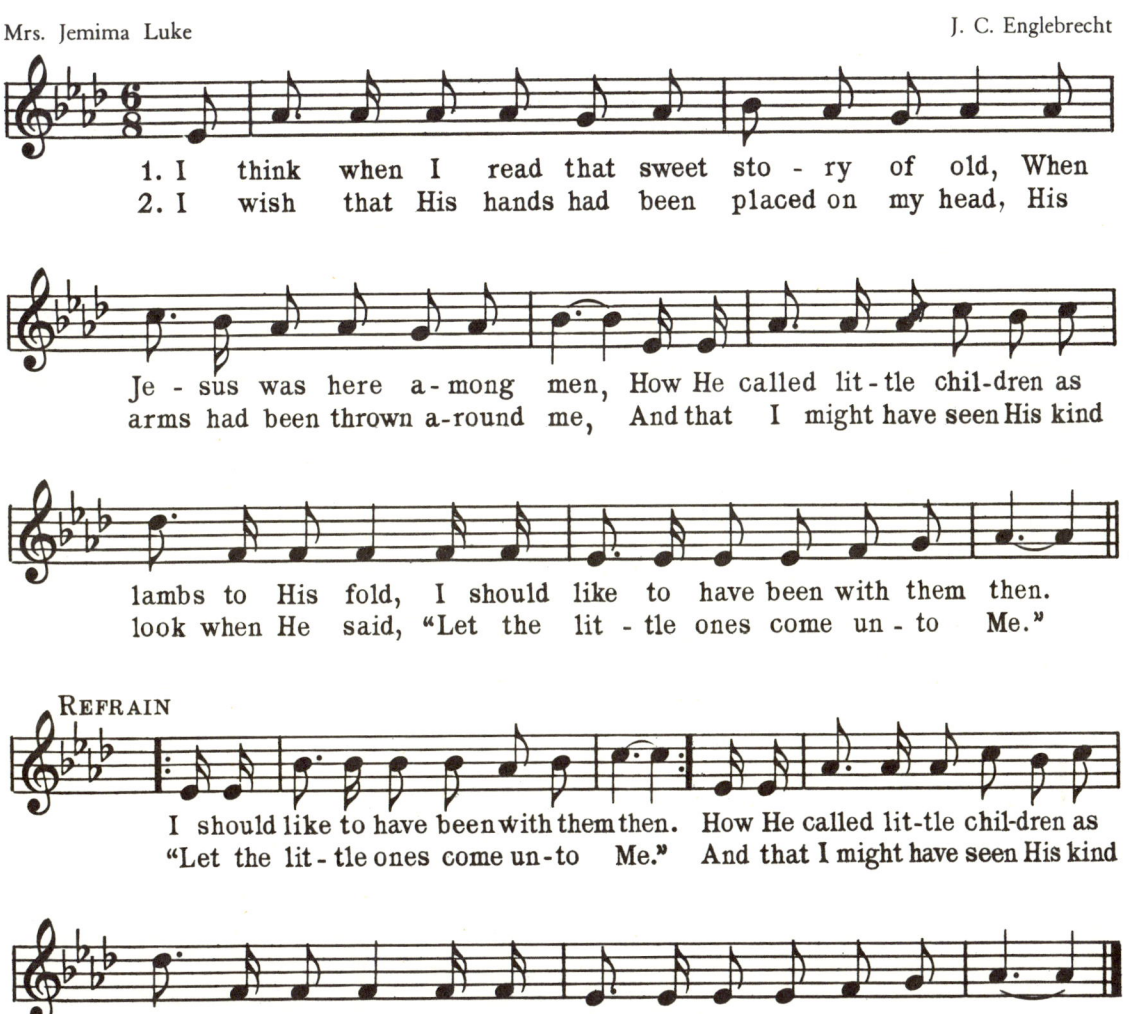

1. I think when I read that sweet sto-ry of old, When Je-sus was here a-mong men, How He called lit-tle chil-dren as lambs to His fold, I should like to have been with them then.
2. I wish that His hands had been placed on my head, His arms had been thrown a-round me, And that I might have seen His kind look when He said, "Let the lit-tle ones come un-to Me."

REFRAIN

I should like to have been with them then. How He called lit-tle chil-dren as lambs to His fold, I should like to have been with them then.
"Let the lit-tle ones come un-to Me." And that I might have seen His kind look when He said, "Let the lit-tle ones come un-to Me."

Gracious Saviour, Gentle Shepherd

Jane E. Lesson
John B. Dykes

1. Gra-cious Sav-iour, gen-tle Shep-herd, Lit-tle ones are dear to Thee;
2. Ten-der Shep-herd, nev-er leave us From Thy fold to go a-stray;
3. Taught to lisp the ho-ly prais-es Which on earth Thy chil-dren sing,

Gath-ered with Thine arms, and car-ried In Thy bo-som may we be.
By Thy look of love di-rect-ed May we walk the nar-row way.
May we with Thy saints in glo-ry Join to praise our Lord and King.

Let Me Learn of Jesus

Fanny J. Crosby
J. F. Swift

1. Let me learn of Je-sus; He is kind to me;
2. If I go to Je-sus, He will hear me pray,
3. Oh, how good is Je-sus! May He hold my hand

Once He died to save me, Nailed up-on the tree.
Make me pure and ho-ly, Take my sins a-way.
And at last re-ceive me To a bet-ter land.

From Music Reader for Lutheran Schools. Used by permission of Concordia Publishing House.

Saviour, Like a Shepherd Lead Us

Mary A. S. Barber Wm. B. Bradbury

1. Sav-iour, like a shep-herd lead us, Much we need Thy ten-d'rest care;
2. We are Thine, do Thou be-friend us, Be the guard-ian of our way;
3. Thou hast prom-ised to re-ceive us, Poor and sin-ful tho' we be;
4. Ear-ly let us seek Thy fa-vor, Ear-ly let us do Thy will;

In Thy pleas-ant pas-tures feed us, For our use Thy folds pre-pare;
Keep Thy flock, from sin de-fend us, Seek us when we go a-stray;
Thou hast mer-cy to re-lieve us, Grace to cleanse, and pow'r to free:
Bless-ed Lord and on-ly Sav-iour, With Thy love our bos-oms fill:

Bless-ed Je-sus! Bless-ed Je-sus! Thou hast bought us, Thine we are,
Bless-ed Je-sus! Bless-ed Je-sus! Hear, O hear us, when we pray,
Bless-ed Je-sus! Bless-ed Je-sus! We will ear-ly turn to Thee.
Bless-ed Je-sus! Bless-ed Je-sus! Thou hast loved us, love us still.

Bless-ed Jesus! Bless-ed Jesus! Thou hast bought us, Thine we are.
Bless-ed Jesus! Bless-ed Jesus! Hear, O hear us, when we pray.
Bless-ed Jesus! Bless-ed Jesus! We will ear-ly turn to Thee.
Bless-ed Jesus! Bless-ed Jesus! Thou hast loved us, love us still.

God's Love Eternal

From the German
Old German Melody

1. God's love e-ter-nal, Planned my re-demp-tion, God's bound-less mer-cy Sought e-ven me!
2. God's love sent Je-sus, The faith-ful Sav-iour, To seek and save me From sin and death.

REFRAIN

There-fore re-joice and praise His bound-less mer-cy; His love e-ter-nal Saves e-ven me.

From MUSIC READER for *Lutheran Schools*. Used by permission of Concordia Publishing House.

There Is a Green Hill Far Away

Mrs. Cecil F. Alexander   John H. Gower

1. There is a green hill far a-way, With-out a cit-y wall,
   Where the dear Lord was cru-ci-fied, Who died to save us all.
2. We may not know, we can-not tell, What pains He had to bear;
   But we be-lieve it was for us He hung and suf-fered there.
3. He died that we might be for-giv'n, He died to make us good,
   That we might go at last to heav'n, Saved by His pre-cious blood.
4. There was no oth-er good e-nough To pay the price of sin;
   He on-ly could un-lock the gate Of heav'n, and let us in.
5. O dear-ly, dear-ly has He loved, And we must love Him too,
   And trust in His re-deem-ing blood, And try His works to do.

Copyright by John H. Gower. By permission.

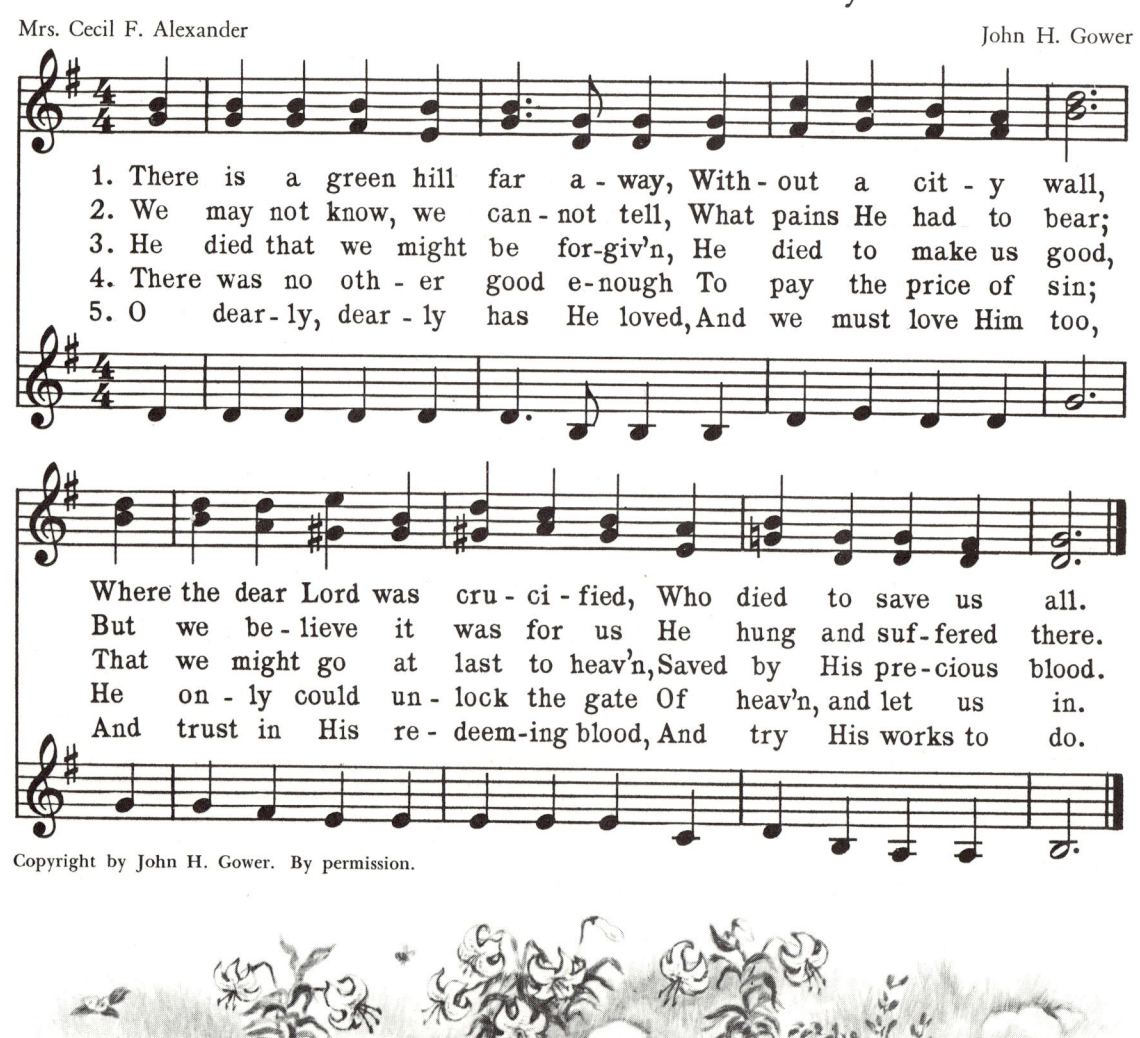

At the Dawn of Easter Day

Ruth Heller
Old Easter Chorale Adapted and Arranged by R.H.

1. At the dawn of East-er day The an-gels rolled the rock a-way.
2. To His friends the Lord did come; He brought them joy and blessed each one.

Those who thought the Lord was dead Found He was a-live in-stead.
Told them He would al-ways stay. Thank you, God, for East-er Day!

From *Father, Hear Thy Children Sing*, copyright 1953, by Hall & McCreary Company. Used by permission.

Alleluia! Easter Angels

Paul Zellar Strodach
Cörner's *Gesangbuch*

Al-le-lu-ia! East-er an-gels Tell us of the ris-en Lord;

From the grave He came in glo-ry; Ev-er lives to be a-dored!

Used by permission of the Board of Publication of the United Lutheran Church.

Christ the Lord Is Ris'n Today

John Wesley
Davidica

Now Let Us All with One Accord

Frances B. Wood
Melody from *Geistliche Kirchengesänge*

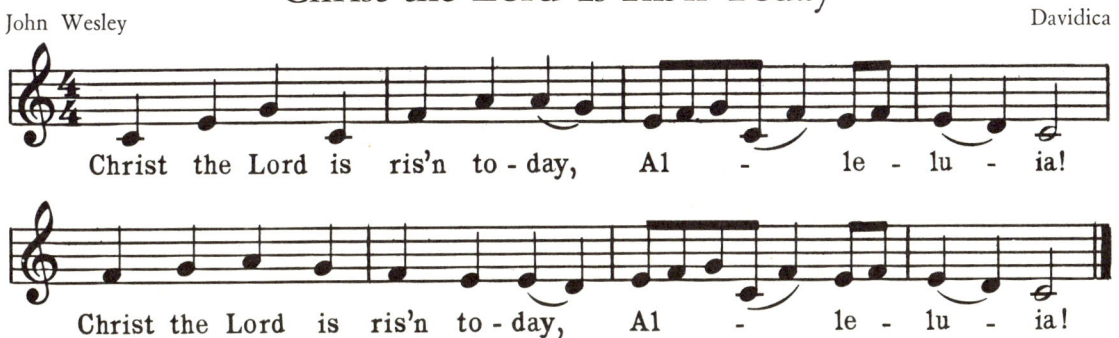

Now let us all with one ac-cord Sing prais-es to our gra-cious Lord, Al-le-lu-ia, Al-le-lu-ia! Who on that first glad East-er Day Rose to re-joice the world al-way, Al-le-lu-ia, Al-le-lu-ia, Al-le-lu-ia! Al-le-lu-ia! Al-le-lu---ia!

Words copyright by Frances B. Wood. Used by permission. Music copyright, 1940, by Presbyterian Board of Christian Education.

Jesus, from Thy Throne on High

T. B. Pollock E. Bunnett

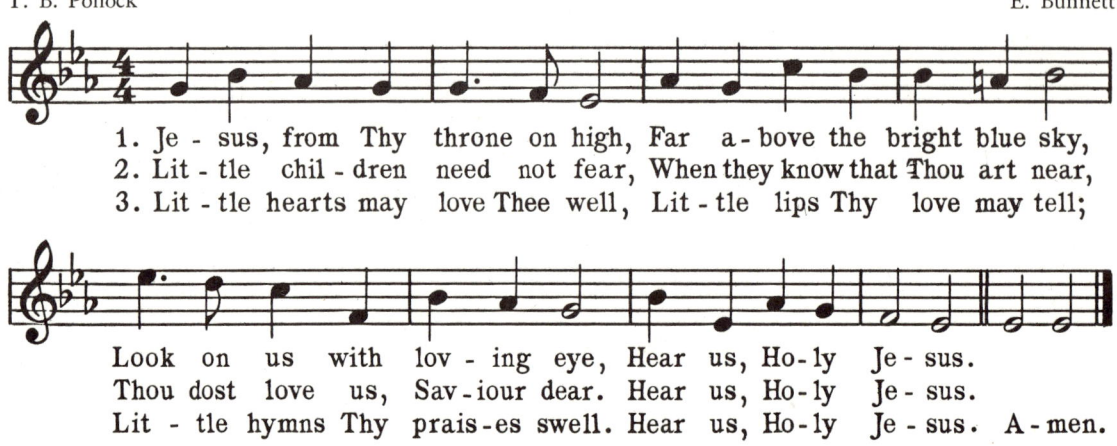

1. Je-sus, from Thy throne on high, Far a-bove the bright blue sky,
Look on us with lov-ing eye, Hear us, Ho-ly Je-sus.
2. Lit-tle chil-dren need not fear, When they know that Thou art near,
Thou dost love us, Sav-iour dear. Hear us, Ho-ly Je-sus.
3. Lit-tle hearts may love Thee well, Lit-tle lips Thy love may tell;
Lit-tle hymns Thy prais-es swell. Hear us, Ho-ly Je-sus. A-men.

Words used by permission. This music is the copyright of the composer, and is inserted by his permission.

There Is a Happy Land

Andrew Young Indian Melody

There is a hap-py land, Far, far a-way, Where saints in glo-ry stand, Bright, bright as day. O how they sweet-ly sing, "Wor-thy is our Sav-iour King," Loud let His prais-es ring, Praise, praise for aye!

Jewels

W. O. Cushing
Geo. F. Root

1. When He com-eth, when He com-eth To make up His jew-els,
2. He will gath-er, He will gath-er The gems for His king-dom;
3. Lit-tle chil-dren, lit-tle chil-dren, Who love their Re-deem-er,

All His jew-els, pre-cious jew-els, His loved and His own.
All the pure ones, all the bright ones, His loved and His own.
Are the jew-els, pre-cious jew-els, His loved and His own.

REFRAIN

Like the stars of the morn-ing, His bright crown a-dorn-ing,

They shall shine in their beau-ty, Bright gems for His crown.

Lord, Who Lovest Little Children

M.R.   Adapted from Novello

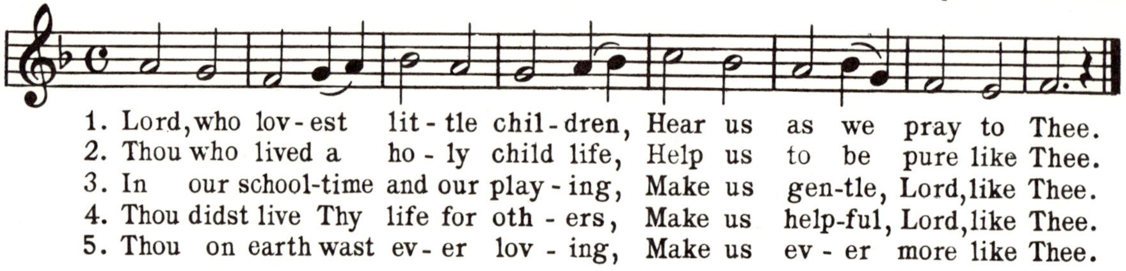

1. Lord, who lovest little children, Hear us as we pray to Thee.
2. Thou who lived a holy child life, Help us to be pure like Thee.
3. In our school-time and our playing, Make us gentle, Lord, like Thee.
4. Thou didst live Thy life for others, Make us helpful, Lord, like Thee.
5. Thou on earth wast ever loving, Make us evermore like Thee.

Copyright by Judson Press. Used by permission.

A Prayer to Jesus

Frances Weld Danielson   Henry Baker

Lord Jesus, may I always be Tender and kind of heart like Thee;
If any suffer or are sad, Help me to try to make them glad.

From *Songs for Little People*, by Danielson and Conant. Copyright, the Pilgrim Press. Used by permission.

Fairest Lord Jesus

From German

98

All Glory, Laud and Honor

"Hosanna!" Be the Children's Song

James Montgomery
Gesangbuch der Herzogl

"Ho-san-na!" be the chil-dren's song To Christ, the chil-dren's King;

His praise, to whom they all be-long, Let all the chil-dren sing.

REFRAIN

"Ho-san-na!" then, our song shall be; "Ho-san-na to our King!"

This is the chil-dren's ju-bi-lee; Let all the chil-dren sing.

Little Children, Praise the Saviour

From the Juvenile Harmonist
From George Frederick Handel

1. Lit-tle chil-dren, praise the Sav-iour, He re-gards you from a-bove;
2. When He left His home in glo-ry, When He lived with peo-ple here,

Praise Him for His great sal-va-tion, Praise Him for His pre-cious love.
Lit-tle chil-dren sang His prais-es, And it pleased His gra-cious ear.

CHORUS
Sweet ho-san-nas, sweet ho-san-nas To the name of Je-sus sing;

Sweet ho-san-nas, sweet ho-san-nas To the name of Je-sus sing.

I Would Follow Jesus

Frank von Christierson Roberta Bitgood

I would fol-low Je-sus, Teach-er, Friend, and Guide;
In my work and in my play, In my home and school each day,
In God's world so fair and wide, I would fol-low Je-sus.

Words and arrangement from *Hymns for Primary Worship*. Copyright 1946 by the Westminster Press. Used by permission.

A Child's Prayer

L.P. III Lillian Payson

1. Ho-ly Spir-it, come and stay With a hum-ble child I pray;
2. Pre-cious Sav-iour, come and stay With Thy lov-ing child I pray;
3. Heav'n-ly Fa-ther, come and stay With Thy child by night and day;

Make me like the pure a-bove, Fill my heart with peace and love.
Good and true, oh! let me be; Mild and gen-tle, Lord, like Thee.
Teach me all Thy will to do; Make me love to please Thee too.

By permission David C. Cook Publishing Company.

All for Jesus, All for Jesus

William John Sparrow Simpson John Stainer

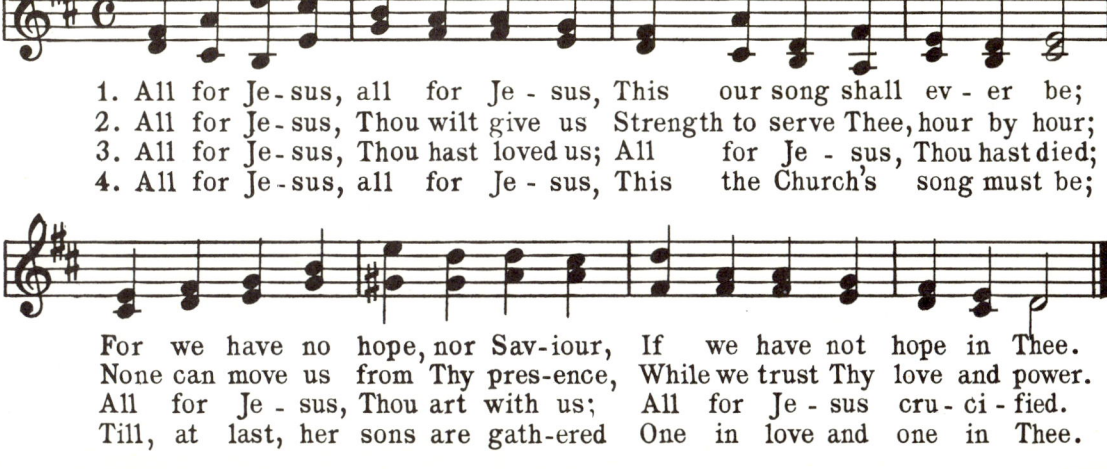

1. All for Je-sus, all for Je-sus, This our song shall ev-er be;
2. All for Je-sus, Thou wilt give us Strength to serve Thee, hour by hour;
3. All for Je-sus, Thou hast loved us; All for Je-sus, Thou hast died;
4. All for Je-sus, all for Je-sus, This the Church's song must be;

For we have no hope, nor Sav-iour, If we have not hope in Thee.
None can move us from Thy pres-ence, While we trust Thy love and power.
All for Je-sus, Thou art with us; All for Je-sus cru-ci-fied.
Till, at last, her sons are gath-ered One in love and one in Thee.

Anywhere with Jesus

Jessie H. Brown and Ruth Heller
D. B. Towner

1. An-y-where with Je-sus I'll be safe, I know;
2. An-y-where with Je-sus I've a friend that's true;

An-y-where He leads me, I'll not fear to go.
An-y-where with Je-sus, He will see me through.

Though the sun is hid-ing or is shin-ing bright,
Though I can-not see Him, He is at my side.

With my hand in His hand, things will be all right.
An-y-where is safe if Je-sus is my guide.

From *Father, Hear Thy Children Sing*, copyright 1953, by Hall & McCreary Company. Used by permission.

Two Little Hands

W.A.O.
W. A. Ogden

1. I've two lit-tle hands to work for Je-sus, One lit-tle tongue His praise to tell,
2. I've two lit-tle feet to tread the path-way Up to the heav'n-ly courts a-bove;
3. I've one lit-tle heart to give to Je-sus, One lit-tle soul for Him to save,

Two lit-tle ears to hear His coun-sel, One lit-tle voice a song to swell.
Two lit-tle eyes to read the Bi-ble, Tell-ing of Je-sus' won-drous love.
One lit-tle life for His dear serv-ice, One lit-tle self that He must have.

CHORUS

Lord, we come, Lord, we come, In our child-hood's ear-ly morn-ing;

Lord, we come, Lord, we come, Come to learn of Thee.

By permission David C. Cook Publishing Company.

105

I Give Thee My Hands

Florence O'Keane Whelan
F.O.W.

I give Thee my hands, Dear Jesus, And all the work they do. I give Thee my heart, Dear Jesus. My love for Thee is true.

From *Father, Hear Thy Children Sing*, copyright 1953, by Hall & McCreary Company. Used by permission.

Book Divine

John Burton, Jr.
Xavier Schneider von Wartenesee

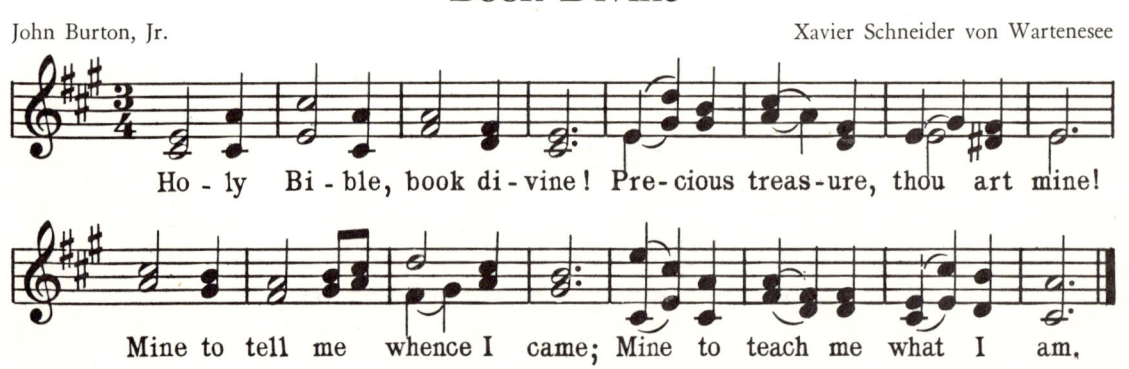

Holy Bible, book divine! Precious treasure, thou art mine! Mine to tell me whence I came; Mine to teach me what I am.

For Stories Fine and True

Ethel L. Smither
Melchior Teschner

We thank Thee, O our Father, For stories fine and true

Of people in the Bi - ble Who knew and loved Thee too.
They learned to serve Thee brave - ly, To help 'gainst pain and wrong;
They wondered at Thy good - ness; They praised in joy - ous song.

Words used by permission of Ethel L. Smither.

The Bible Helps Me

Mabel Niedermeyer   Adapted from *Day's Psalter*

1. The Bi - ble helps me know the Friend Of chil - dren ev - ery-where,
2. I like the sto - ries that it tells Of Je - sus do - ing good;

Who came to help us un - der-stand Our Fa - ther's love and care.
They help me act in friend - ly ways To do the things I should.

Words from *Hymns for Primary Worship*. Copyright 1946 by the Westminster Press. Used by permission.

Little Moses

Roberta L. Best R.L.B.

1. Dear little baby Moses, Sleeping so cozy and warm, Hidden in the rushes To keep you safe from harm.
2. Dear little baby Moses, Your sister is watching nearby; Pharaoh must not find you, Do not wake and cry.
3. Dear little baby Moses, You are God's chosen one; Pharaoh's daughter will find you, And you will be her son.

From *Father, Hear Thy Children Sing*, copyright 1953, by Hall & McCreary Company. Used by permission.

Dare to Be a Daniel

P. P. Bliss P.P.B.

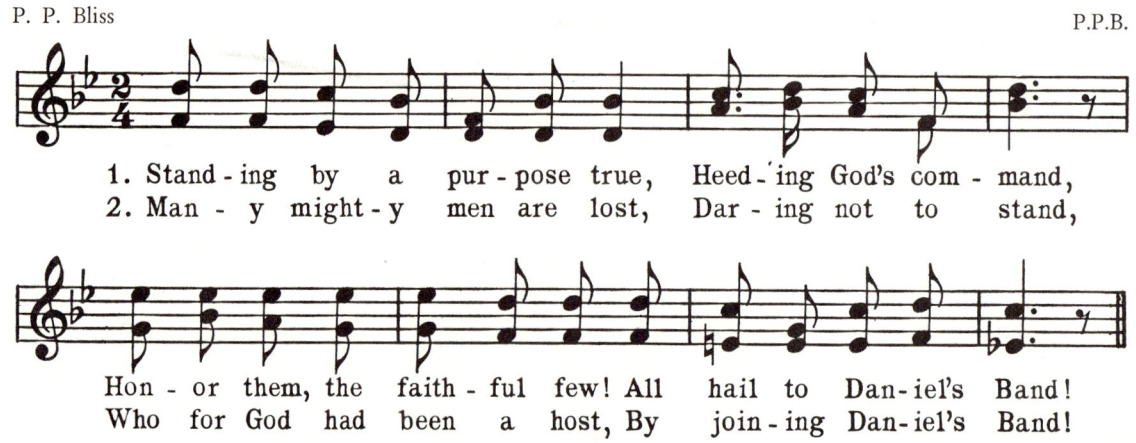

1. Standing by a purpose true, Heeding God's command, Honor them, the faithful few! All hail to Daniel's Band!
2. Many mighty men are lost, Daring not to stand, Who for God had been a host, By joining Daniel's Band!

CHORUS

Dare to be a Daniel, Dare to stand a-lone,
Dare to have a pur-pose firm! Dare to make it known!

Happy Hearts

Laneta Wilson
C. A. Fyke

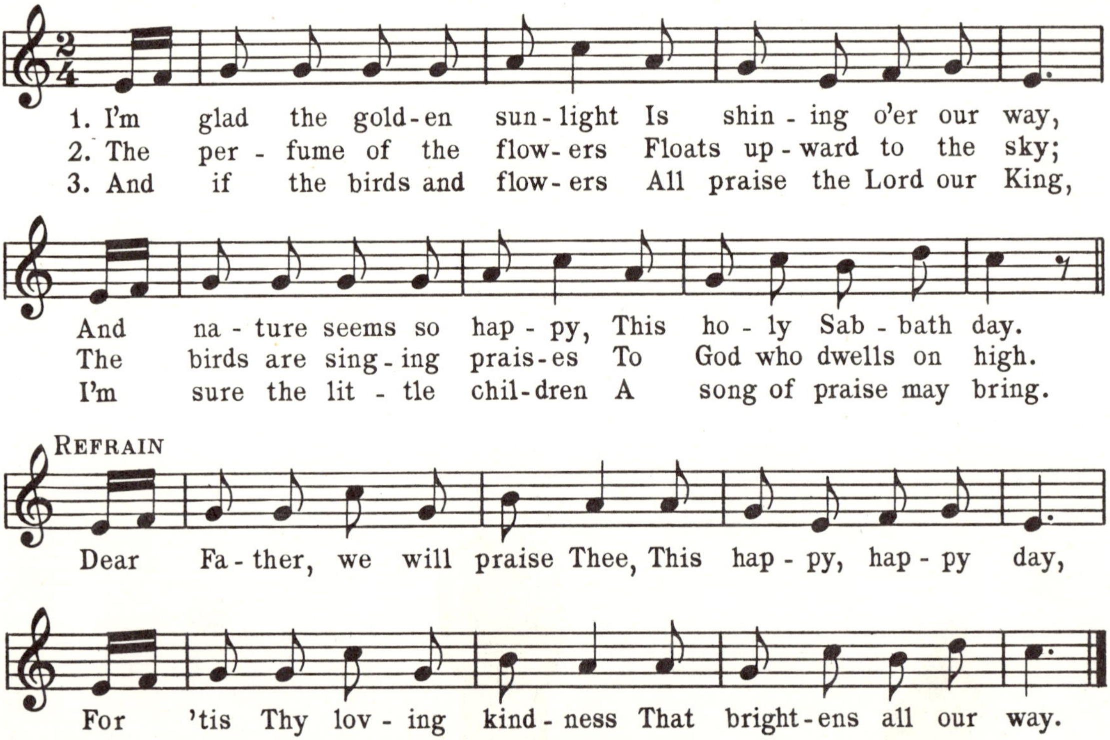

1. I'm glad the gold-en sun-light Is shin-ing o'er our way,
2. The per-fume of the flow-ers Floats up-ward to the sky;
3. And if the birds and flow-ers All praise the Lord our King,

And na-ture seems so hap-py, This ho-ly Sab-bath day.
The birds are sing-ing prais-es To God who dwells on high.
I'm sure the lit-tle chil-dren A song of praise may bring.

REFRAIN

Dear Fa-ther, we will praise Thee, This hap-py, hap-py day,

For 'tis Thy lov-ing kind-ness That bright-ens all our way.

Copyright by David C. Cook Publishing Co. Used by permission. From *Primary Songs No. 1*.

I Was Glad When They Said unto Me

Psalm 122:1
Roberta Bitgood

I was glad when they said un-to me, Let us go un-to the house of the Lord.

Music from *Hymns for Primary Worship*, copyright, 1946, by the Westminster Press. Used by permission.

110

This Is the Day the Lord Hath Made

Isaac Watts T. A. Arne

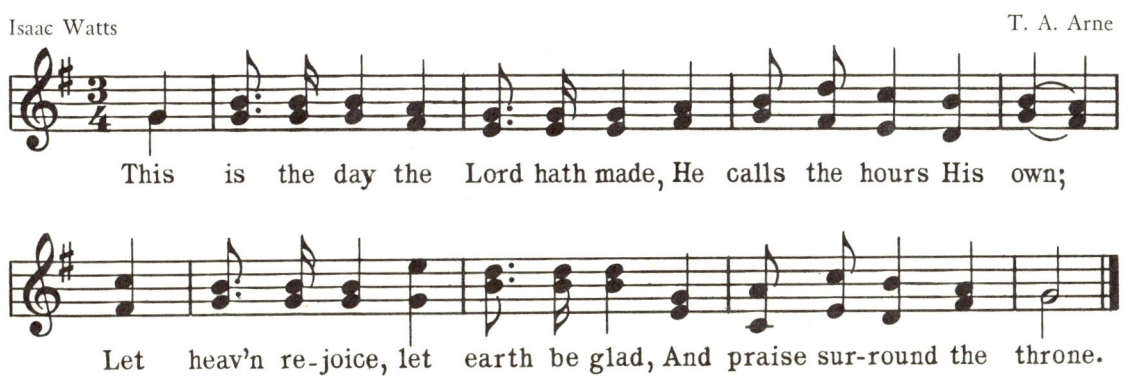

This is the day the Lord hath made, He calls the hours His own;
Let heav'n re-joice, let earth be glad, And praise sur-round the throne.

When to Church I Go

Caroline Kellogg Dorothy West

Ver-y soft-ly I will walk, Ver-y gen-tly I will talk, When to church I go.
Though I can-not see Him there, God is with me ev-'ry-where; He is here, I know.

Used by permission of the American Baptist Publication Society.

Enter into His Gates

Nettie Delphine Ellsworth

En-ter in-to His gates with thanks-giv-ing, And in-to His courts with praise;
Be thank-ful un-to Him, and bless His name, For the Lord is good.

By permission of Emma S. Dietz.

Praise the Lord

C.E.P.
Charles Edw. Pollock

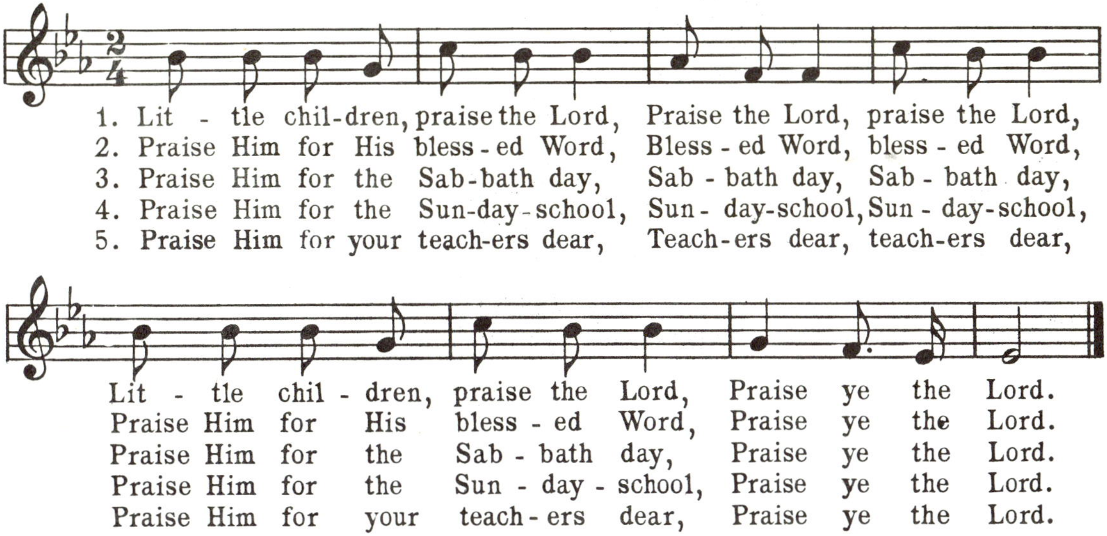

1. Lit - tle chil-dren, praise the Lord, Praise the Lord, praise the Lord,
2. Praise Him for His bless-ed Word, Bless-ed Word, bless-ed Word,
3. Praise Him for the Sab-bath day, Sab-bath day, Sab-bath day,
4. Praise Him for the Sun-day-school, Sun-day-school, Sun-day-school,
5. Praise Him for your teach-ers dear, Teach-ers dear, teach-ers dear,

Lit - tle chil - dren, praise the Lord, Praise ye the Lord.
Praise Him for His bless - ed Word, Praise ye the Lord.
Praise Him for the Sab - bath day, Praise ye the Lord.
Praise Him for the Sun - day - school, Praise ye the Lord.
Praise Him for your teach - ers dear, Praise ye the Lord.

By permission David C. Cook Pub. Co.

We Love Our Church, O God

Stanza 1, Nan F. Heflin
Stanza 2, Clara Beers Blashfield

A. Williams' *Psalmody*

1. We love our church, O God, We love to gather here To worship, work, and learn of Thee With Christian friends so dear.
2. We love our church, O God, This place of friendly cheer; We come to sing, to work, to pray To God who is ever near.

From *Song Friends for Younger Children.* Copyright 1932 by Clara Beers Blashfield. Used by permission of the publishers, the Vaile Company. Stanza 1 copyright 1942 by the American Baptist Publication Society. Used by permission.

Here in Our Father's House

Mrs. C. B. Palmer and Dorothy F. Poulton

Lowell Mason

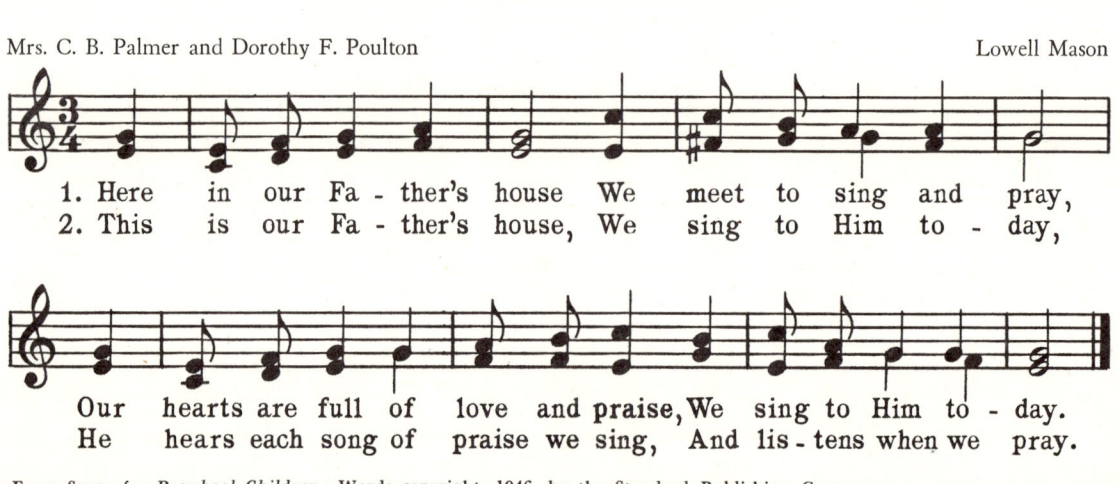

1. Here in our Father's house We meet to sing and pray, Our hearts are full of love and praise, We sing to Him today.
2. This is our Father's house, We sing to Him today, He hears each song of praise we sing, And listens when we pray.

From *Songs for Preschool Children.* Words copyright, 1946, by the Standard Publishing Company.

Closing Prayer

Mary B. Blakemore

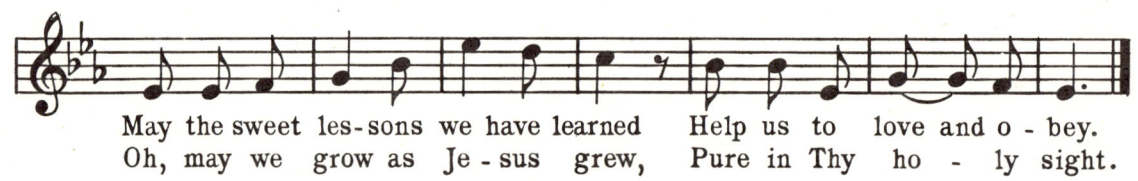

1. Dear Father, bless us as we go Each on his homeward way,
   May the sweet lessons we have learned Help us to love and obey.
2. Dear Father, help us day by day Bravely to do the right,
   Oh, may we grow as Jesus grew, Pure in Thy holy sight.

May the Grace of Christ, Our Saviour

J. Newton J. Thommen

1. May the grace of Christ, our Saviour, And the Father's boundless love
   With the Holy Spirit's favor, Rest upon us from above.
2. Thus may we abide in union With each other and the Lord
   And possess in sweet communion Joys which earth cannot afford.

From MUSIC READER *for Lutheran Schools.* Used by permission of Concordia Publishing House.

To Thy Father and Thy Mother

Anne Ross Cousin
Ludwig and Witt's *Psalmodia Sacra*

To thy fa-ther and thy moth-er Hon-or, love, and rev-'rence pay;

This com-mand, be-fore all oth-er, Must a Chris-tian child o-bey.

Honor Thy Father and Mother

Louise M. Oglevee
William G. Oglevee

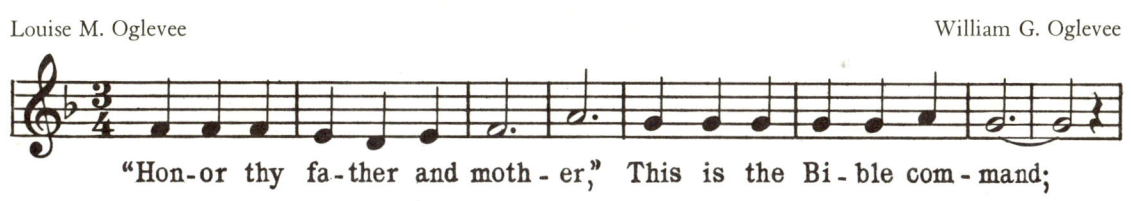

"Hon-or thy fa-ther and moth-er," This is the Bi-ble com-mand;

"Then shalt thou live long and pros-per, In this, thy God-giv-en land."

Home

F. A. Jackson
From F. Silcher

1. O Fa-ther, our dear Fa-ther, For all the love we see, For
2. For home and all its beau-ty, For gra-cious thought and word, For

par-ents, broth-er, sis-ter, We bring our thanks to Thee, We bring our thanks to Thee.
all the peace and glad-ness, We thank Thee, thank Thee, Lord! We thank Thee, thank Thee, Lord!

Words copyright by the National Sunday School Union. Used by permission.

Mother's Day

Mabel V. K. Ballard, 1st stanza
Edith Lovell Thomas, 2nd and 3rd stanzas
Juniors, First Presbyterian Church School, Gloversville, N.Y.

1. All through the year we'll try to do The things that show our love for you;
2. How could we live with-out you near To guide us through the times of fear?
3. Thanks un-to God to-day we give For homes where loy-al fam-i-lies live;

We'll not be hap-py just to say, "We love you, Moth-er," on Moth-er's Day.
Ill or in health you take your share In all the pleas-ure and pain we bear.
Hon-or to them who keep them true The moth-er, fa-ther, and chil-dren too.

Words used by permission of the authors, Mabel V. K. Ballard and Edith Lovell Thomas. Tune contributed by the composers.

Love One Another

Mattie C. Leatherwood — Mildred Adair Stagg

1. Love one an-oth-er, Love one an-oth-er,
2. Help one an-oth-er, Help one an-oth-er,
3. Share with one an-oth-er, Share with one an-oth-er,

This is the hap-py way, Love one an-oth-er.
This is the hap-py way, Help one an-oth-er.
This is the hap-py way, Share with one an-oth-er.

Copyright, 1939, by the Sunday School Board of the Southern Baptist Convention. Used by permission.

The Golden Rule

Emerson and Tilden

Be to oth-ers ev-er kind and ev-er true,
As you'd have them ev-er faith-ful be to you.

From *New Music Horizons*, Book IV. Used by special permission of Silver Burdett Company, New York.

Little Things

1. Lit - tle drops of wa - ter, Lit - tle grains of sand,
2. Lit - tle deeds of kind - ness, Lit - tle words of love,

Make the might - y o - cean, And the pleas - ant land.
Help to make earth hap - py, Like the heav - en a - bove.

From *New Music Horizons,* Book I. Used by special permission of Silver Burdett Company, New York.

God Wants Us to Be Cheerful

Ruth Heller
German Folk Song

God wants us to be cheer-ful In our work and in our play,

God wants us to be thought-ful And help oth-ers ev-'ry day.

God wants us to be friend-ly And He wants us to be good.

We show how much we love Him When we do the things we should.

From *Father, Hear Thy Children Sing*, copyright 1953, by Hall & McCreary Company. Used by permission.

We Are All God's Little Children

Ruth Heller
John Stainer

We are all God's lit-tle chil-dren. He is Fa-ther of us all.
He in heav-en watch-es o'er us, Loves His chil-dren, big and small.

From *Father, Hear Thy Children Sing*, copyright 1953, by Hall & McCreary Company. Used by permission.

We Pray for Children o'er the Sea

Florence O'Keane Whelan
Old Tune

We pray for chil-dren o'er the sea, God bless them ev-'ry one.
May they learn of Je-sus, Thine own be-lov-ed Son.

From *Father, Hear Thy Children Sing*, copyright 1953, by Hall & McCreary Company. Used by permission.

God's World

Nancy Byrd Turner
Polish Folk Song

1. All the world is God's world; So we kneel and pray,
2. "When our sun is shin-ing, And our land is bright,
3. "When our day is o-ver, And our twi-light comes,

"Bless the oth-er chil-dren Far and far a-way!"
Their land's in the shad-ow, Keep them through the night!"
They are see-ing sun-rise. Bless them in their homes!"

Words used by permission of Nancy Byrd Turner. From *The Whole World Singing*, by Edith Lovell Thomas. Friendship Press.

Once Again, Dear Lord, We Pray

M. J. Wilcox
Justin H. Knecht

1. Once a-gain, dear Lord, we pray For the chil-dren far a-way,
2. Lit-tle lips that Thou hast made, 'Neath the far-off tem-ple's shade
3. Lit-tle hands, whose won-drous skill Thou hast giv'n to do Thy will,
4. Teach them, O Thou heav'n-ly King, All their gifts and praise to bring

Who have nev-er e-ven heard Name of Je-sus, sweet-est word.
Give to gods of wood and stone Praise that should be all Thine own.
Of-f'rings bring, and serve with fear Gods that can-not see or hear.
To Thy Son, who died to prove Thy for-giv-ing, sav-ing love.

The Many, Many Children

Wilhelmina D'A Stephens   Lowell Mason

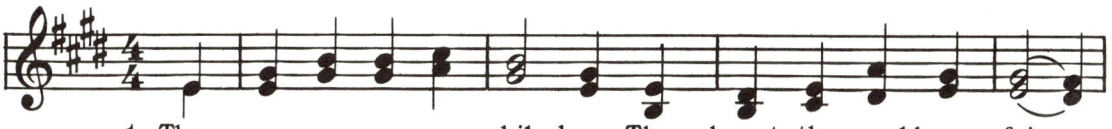

1. The man-y, man-y chil-dren Through-out the world so fair
2. Then let us, all His chil-dren, At home, at work, at play,

Are chil-dren of our Fa-ther, Who keeps them in His care.
Be quick to help each oth-er, Our Fa-ther's will o-bey,

No mat-ter what their col-or, He loves them one and all;
That all the wide world's chil-dren In hap-pi-ness may live,

No mat-ter where they're liv-ing, He hears them when they call.
What-e'er their race or col-or, And praise to Him may give.

From *Beginners' Teachers' Quarterly.* Copyright 1929 by the Presbyterian Board of Education. Second stanza from *Hymns for Primary Worship.* Copyright 1946 by the Westminster Press. Used by permission.

True Neighbors

Ernest Bourner Allen
Edith Lovell Thomas

We send our love to eve-ry land; True neigh-bors we would be;
And pray God's peace to reign in them, Wher-e'er their home-land be.
O God, to us may grace be given, Who bear the dear Christ's name,
To live at peace with eve-ry man, And thus our Christ ac-claim.

Words used by permission of Mrs. Ernest Bourner Allen. Music copyright, 1935, by Edith Lovell Thomas.

Thanksgiving

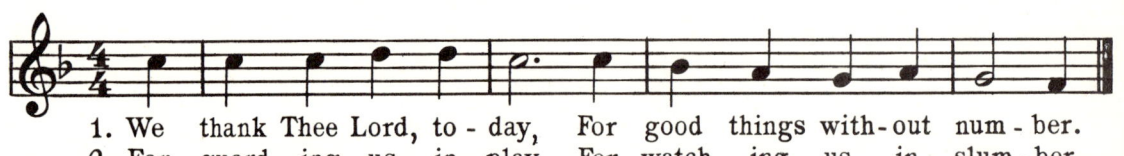

1. We thank Thee Lord, to-day, For good things with-out num-ber.
2. For guard-ing us in play, For watch-ing us in slum-ber.

From *Our Songs.* Used by permission of C. C. Birchard & Company.

Morning Prayer
I

Elizabeth S. Whitehouse — W. Lawrence Curry

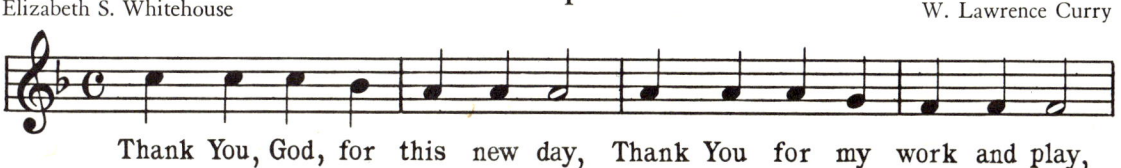

Thank You, God, for this new day, Thank You for my work and play,
For Your care the whole night through, Thank You, God, for all You do.

Words and music from *When a Little Child Wants to Sing*, copyright, 1935, by the Presbyterian Board of Christian Education. Used by permission.

God's Gift of Day and Night

Ida F. Leyda — Fanny B. Earle

1. In the early morning, Dark shadows stay,
   Till the sunbeams bring us God's gift of day.
2. When the day is ended, Stars shining bright
   Bring to tired children God's gift of night.
3. Father, now we thank Thee For morning light,
   For our days of gladness, For rest of night.

By permission of Emma S. Dietz.

Thanks to God

From the Portuguese
By Antonio de Campos Goncalves

Brazilian Folk Song

1. In the morn-ing when I wak-en, As I kneel and make my prayer,
2. When at night the stars are shin-ing, Man-y chil-dren far and near,

I give thanks to God, the Fa-ther, For His ten-der love and care.
Talk with God and ask His bless-ing, Sleep in peace and know no fear.

The melody comes from the central section of the country and was the first tune to be used in the New Evangelical Hymn Book of Brazil.

Children's Chorale

Author unknown

Johann Sebastian Bach

1. For this new morn-ing with its light, For rest and shel-ter
2. For health and food, for love and friends, For ev-'ry-thing Thy

of the night, O Lord of all, we thank Thee.
good-ness sends, O Lord of all, we thank Thee.

From *Music Hour*, Book I. Used by special permission of Silver Burdett Company, New York.

Morning Hymn

Anonymous
Robert W. Gibb

I

1. For flow'rs that bloom a-bout our feet,
2. For this new morn-ing with its light,

For ten-der grass so fresh and sweet;
For rest and shel-ter through the night;

For song of bird and hum of bee;
For health and food, for love and friends;

For all things fair we hear or see,
For ev-'ry-thing Thy good-ness sends,

Fa-ther in heav'n, we thank Thee.
Fa-ther in heav'n, we thank Thee.

Melody and words from *Songs of Many Lands* of THE WORLD OF MUSIC, copyright 1936, 1943. Used by permission of Ginn and Company, owner of the copyright.

Father, We Thank Thee
First Tune

Father, We Thank Thee

Rebecca J. Weston — Second Tune — D. Batchellor, Arranged by Ruth Heller

1. Fa - ther, we thank Thee for the night, And for the pleas-ant morn-ing light, For rest and food and lov-ing care, And all that makes the day so fair.
2. Help us to do the things we should, To be to oth-ers kind and good; In all our work and all our play, To love Thee bet-ter eve-ry day.

From *Father, Hear Thy Children Sing*, copyright 1953, by Hall & McCreary Company. Used by permission.

Morning Song

1. Bless-ed Lord of night and morn-ing, Keep us safe from harm this day.
2. Work-ing, play-ing, may we please Thee, Kind in all we do and say.

From *The American Singer*, Book I, by Beattie and Wolverton. Used by permission of American Book Company

I Thank Thee, Lord, for Quiet Rest

Mary L. Duncan Vincent Novello

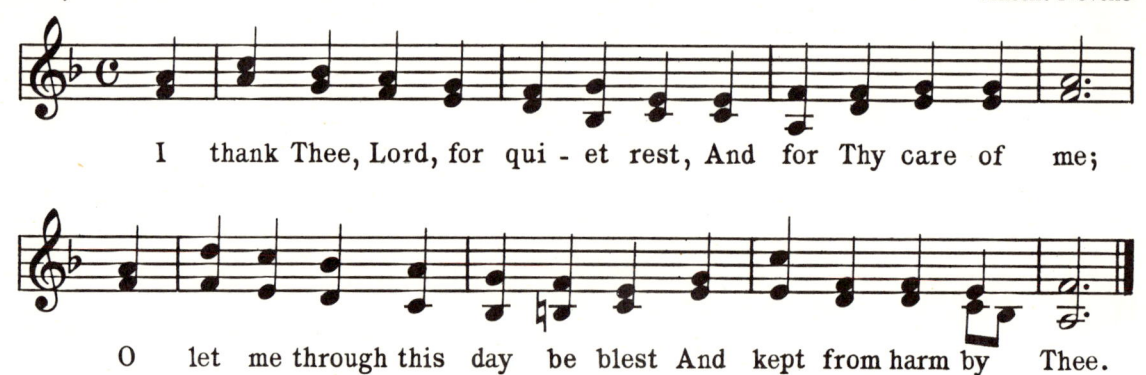

I thank Thee, Lord, for qui-et rest, And for Thy care of me;
O let me through this day be blest And kept from harm by Thee.

A Hymn of Thanks

Charles Ellerton Beethoven

1. Lord, that made the earth and air, We thank Thee for the morn-ing light,
2. Fa-ther dear, we sing to Thee, Who taught the wood-land birds their song;

Thank Thee for the lov-ing care That guards Thy chil-dren thru the night.
God, who made the sky and sea, Pray keep Thy chil-dren all from wrong.

From *New Elementary Music,* by Charles A. Fullerton.

Prayer for Each Day

Elizabeth McE. Shields
Carl Maria von Weber

1. Fa-ther, as the morn-ing sun Lights the world when day's be-gun,
2. As we work and as we play Through each bus-y, hap-py day,
3. Fa-ther, as the eve-ning sun Slow-ly sets when day is done,

May our hearts and voi-ces pray, "Thank You, God, for this good day."
Fa-ther, help us all to be Strong and brave and true like Thee.
May we rest and feel Thy care Guard-ing chil-dren ev-ery-where.

Words from *Primary Music and Worship,* copyright, 1930, by the Presbyterian Board of Christian Education.

A Child's Prayer
IV

Marjorie Knapp
Robert Schumann

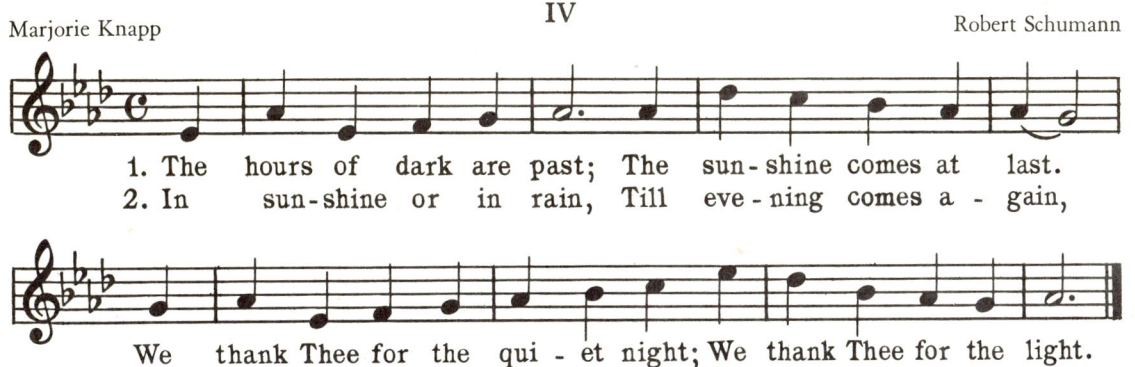

1. The hours of dark are past; The sun-shine comes at last.
2. In sun-shine or in rain, Till eve-ning comes a-gain,

We thank Thee for the qui-et night; We thank Thee for the light.
Both while we work and while we play, Be with us all the day.

From *Listen and Sing,* of The World of Music, copyright, 1936, 1943. Used by permission of Ginn and Company, owner of the copyright.

O God, I Thank Thee for Each Sight

Caroline Atherton Mason Herbert S. Irons

1. O God, I thank Thee for each sight Of beau-ty that Thy hand doth give;
2. That life I con-se-crate to Thee, And ev-er as the day is born,
3. An-oth-er day in which to cast Some si-lent deed of love a-broad,

For sun-ny skies and air and light; O God, I thank Thee that I live.
On wings of joy my soul would flee, And thank Thee for an-oth-er morn;
That, great'ning as it jour-neys past, May do some ear-nest work for God.

The Morning Bright

T. O. Summers English Melody

1. The morn-ing bright With ros-y light Hath waked me from my sleep;
2. All through the day, I hum-bly pray, Be Thou my faith-ful Guide;
3. O make Thy rest With-in my breast, Thou Spir-it of all grace;

O God, I own Thy love a-lone Thy lit-tle one doth keep.
My sins for-give And let me live, Dear Sav-iour, at Thy side.
Make me like Thee, Then shall I be Pre-pared to see Thy face.

From MUSIC READER *for Lutheran Schools.* Used by permission of Concordia Publishing House.

Now I Wake

New England Primer (Adapted) — From Schumann

Now I wake and see the light; God has kept me through the night;
I will lift my eyes and pray: Keep me, Father, through the day.

From *Songs for the Little Child* by Baker and Kohlsaat. Copyright renewal 1949 by Clara Belle Baker. By permission of Abingdon Press.

Morning Prayer

III

Stephen Fay — Harvey W. Loomis

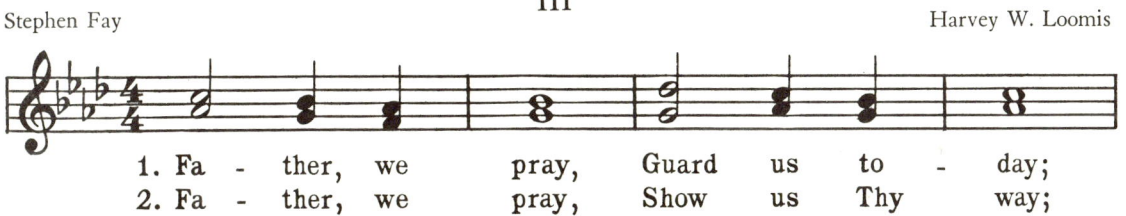

1. Father, we pray, Guard us today;
2. Father, we pray, Show us Thy way;

Keep kindly watch o'er us At work or at play.
Teach us Thy holy Word To hear and obey.

From *We Sing*. Used by permission of C. C. Birchard & Company.

Now the Shades of Night Are Gone

S. Occom J. H. Knecht

1. Now the shades of night are gone, Now the morn-ing light is come.
2. Fill our souls with heav'n-ly light, Ban-ish doubts and cleanse our sight.

Lord, may we be Thine to-day; Drive the shades of sin a-way.
In Thy serv-ice, Lord, to-day Help us la-bor, help us pray.

From MUSIC READER for *Lutheran Schools*. Used by permission of Concordia Publishing House.

Father, Hear Thy Little Children

Alice Jackson J. H. Maunder

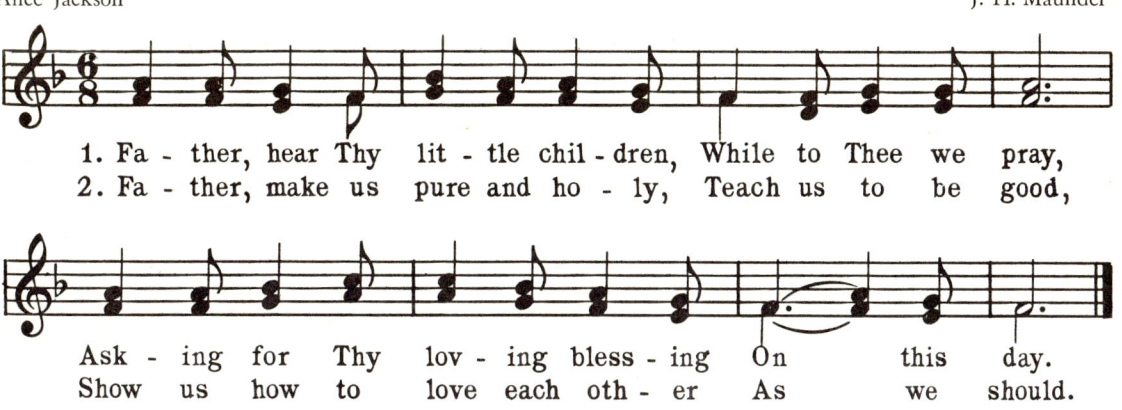

1. Fa-ther, hear Thy lit-tle chil-dren, While to Thee we pray,
2. Fa-ther, make us pure and ho-ly, Teach us to be good,

Ask-ing for Thy lov-ing bless-ing On this day.
Show us how to love each oth-er As we should.

Morning Praise

Nina B. Hartford — Nina B. Hartford

1. Now the day has come a-gain, Night and dark-ness van-ished quite;
   Fa-ther, help us through the day, Guide our foot-steps in the right.
2. We will try to do Thy will, Kind and good and gen-tle be;
   Help-ing oth-ers all we can, Striv-ing thus to live for Thee.

From *Music Hour,* Book IV. Used by special permission of Silver Burdett Company, New York.

Our Father, As We Start the Day

Agnes Kelsey Shute — Henri F. Hemy

Our Fa-ther, as we start the day, We think of chil-dren far a-way
In oth-er lands a-cross the sea. Help us their lov-ing friends to be;
Help all Thy chil-dren ev-ery-where To know Thee and Thy lov-ing care.

Words copyright by Agnes Kelsey Shute. Used by permission.

God's Love

Eliza Graves
Ludwig van Beethoven

1. Oh, let the chil-dren eve-ry-where
2. For e-ven chil-dren un-der-stand

Each morn-ing bow their heads in prayer,
That God, who keeps with lov-ing hand

And ask that God may with them stay,
Each lit-tle bird, each blos-som fair,

And keep them safe-ly through the day.
Will keep His chil-dren eve-ry-where.

From *Music Hour*, Book IV. Used by special permission of Silver Burdett Company, New York.

The Good Shepherd

Kate Cox Goddard
Old Song

1. All day long the shep-herd Guards his lit-tle sheep,
2. God is our good Shep-herd, Cares for eve-ry one,

Herds them in at night-fall, When it's time to sleep.
Watch-es while we're sleep-ing When the day is done.

From *New Music Horizons*, Book III. Used by special permission of Silver Burdett Company, New York.

Evening

Anonymous
Dutch Melody

1. Eve-ning shades are fall-ing, Day-light fades a-way,
2. Al-so lit-tle chil-dren Close their wear-y eyes;

And the world is rest-ing At the close of day.
Ho-ly an-gels guard them Till it's time to rise.

From *Music Reader for Lutheran Schools*. Used by permission of Concordia Publishing House.

God Our Father Watch Will Keep

Grace Wilbur Conant

From *Songs for Little People*, by Danielson and Conant. Copyright, the Pilgrim Press. Used by permission.

Evening Prayer

Eleanor Smith

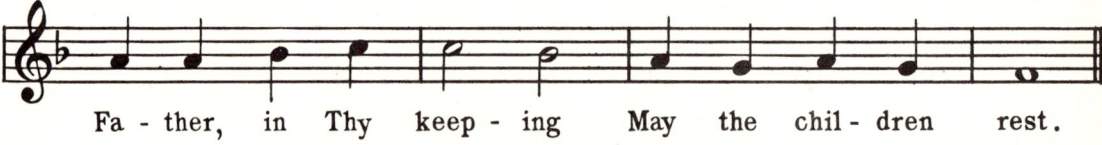

From *Music Hour*, Book I. Used by special permission of Silver Burdett Company, New York.

Day Is Done

Virginia Harrison
Arranged by Lowell Mason from a Gregorian Chant

1. Day now is done, there's a star in the west,
2. When dark is gone and a new day begun,

Still is the land and the twi-light is deep,
Dawn in the sky and a light on the hill,

All things are read-y to turn to their rest,
We shall a-wake and be glad in the sun,

Fa-ther, Thy love is guard-ing our sleep.
Fa-ther, Thy love shall go with us still.

From *New Music Horizons*, Book IV. Used by special permission of Silver Burdett Company, New York.

Now the Day Is Over

S. Baring-Gould
C. H. Rinck

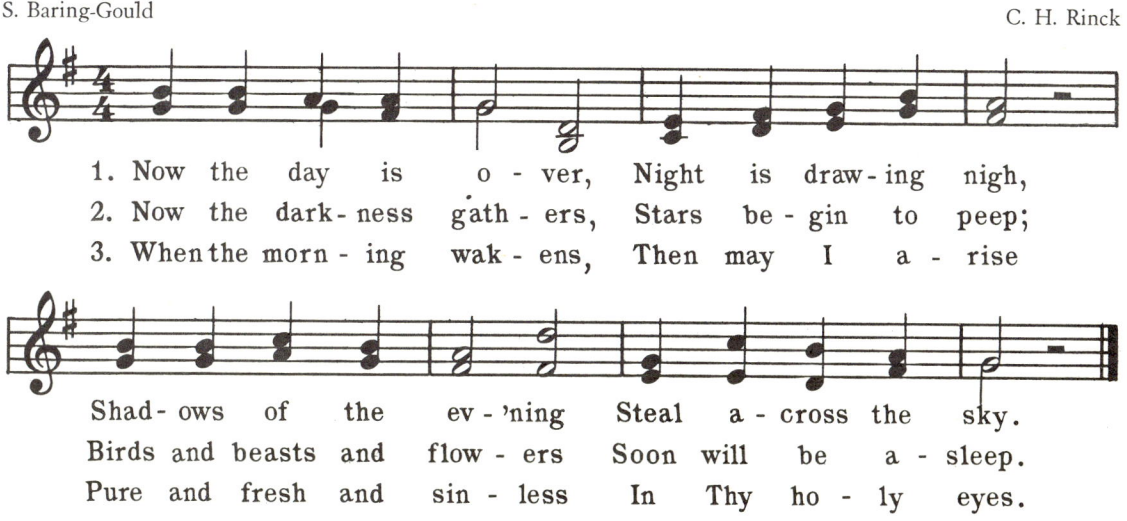

1. Now the day is o-ver, Night is draw-ing nigh,
   Shad-ows of the ev-'ning Steal a-cross the sky.
2. Now the dark-ness gath-ers, Stars be-gin to peep;
   Birds and beasts and flow-ers Soon will be a-sleep.
3. When the morn-ing wak-ens, Then may I a-rise
   Pure and fresh and sin-less In Thy ho-ly eyes.

From *Music Hour*, Book III. Used by special permission of Silver Burdett Company, New York.

Dear Father, Bless Each Little Child

Louise M. Oglevee
William G. Oglevee

Dear Fa-ther, bless each lit-tle child And keep us all, we pray,
Safe in Thy lov-ing care un-til An-oth-er hap-py day.

From *Songs for Little People*, by Danielson and Conant. Copyright by the Pilgrim Press. Used by permission.

A Child's Prayer
V

German Folk Song

1. Soft the shad-ows round me creep, Soon I'll close my eyes in sleep,
2. Keep, O Lord, my friends so dear, All whose love pro-tects me here,

Fa - ther of us all, I pray, Guard my bed till break of day.
Bless all peo-ple great and small, Look in kind-ness on us all.

From *The American Singer*, Book II, by Beattie and Wolverton. Used by permission of American Book Company

An Evening Hymn

Thomas Ken   Thomas Tallis

All praise to Thee, my God, this night, For
all the bless-ings of the light! Keep me, O keep me,
King of kings, Be-neath Thy own al-might-y wings!

A Child's Evensong

John Stainer

1. From the heav'n a-bove us, 'Mid the an-gels mild,
Looks a lov-ing Fa-ther Down on ev-'ry child;
Ten-der-ly He lis-tens When He hears us pray,
Faith-ful-ly He guides us On our earth-ly way.

2. Boun-teous-ly He gives us Food and rai-ment still,
Gra-cious-ly He keeps us From each threat-'ning ill;
Praise the lov-ing Fa-ther, Of His good-ness tell,
He will not for-sake us, He doth love us well.

From *The American Singer*, Book III, by Beattie and Wolverton. Used by permission of American Book Company

Jesus, Tender Shepherd, Hear Me

Mary Lundie Duncan — First Tune — John Stainer

1. Je-sus, ten-der Shep-herd, hear me; Bless Thy lit-tle lamb to-night;
2. Through this day Thy hand has led me, And I thank Thee for Thy care;
3. Let my sins be all for-giv-en; Bless the friends I love so well;

Through the dark-ness be Thou near me, Keep me safe till morn-ing light.
Thou hast warmed me, clothed and fed me, Lis-ten to my eve-ning prayer.
Take me, when I die, to heav-en, Hap-py there with Thee to dwell.

Jesus, Tender Shepherd, Hear Me

Mary Duncan — Second Tune — Wolfgang Amadeus Mozart / Arranged by Ruth Heller

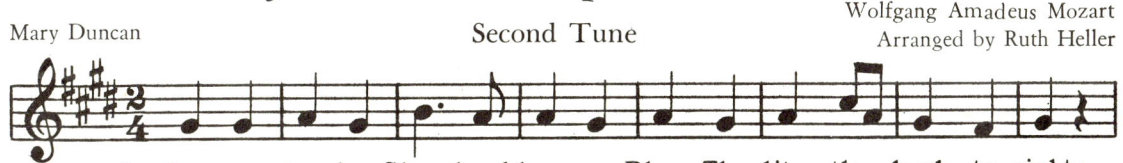

1. Je-sus, ten-der Shep-herd, hear me; Bless Thy lit-tle lamb to-night;
2. All this day Thy hand has led me, And I thank Thee for Thy care;

Through the dark-ness be Thou near me; Keep me safe till morn-ing light.
Thou hast clothed me, warmed and fed me, Lis-ten to my eve-ning prayer.

From *Father, Hear Thy Children Sing*, copyright 1953, by Hall & McCreary Company. Used by permission.

When I Say My Prayer

Roberta L. Best R.L.B.

1. When I say my prayer each night, I kneel be-side my bed,
   I close my eyes and fold my hands And then I bow my head.
2. Thank You, Lord, for ev-'ry-thing, And please help me to be
   As sweet and kind to ev-'ry-one As You have been to me.

From *Father, Hear Thy Children Sing*, copyright 1953, by Hall & McCreary Company. Used by permission.

Evening Hymn

Reginald Heber W. H. Monk

1. God, that mad-est earth and heav-en, Dark-ness and light;
   Who the day for toil hast giv-en, For rest the night.
2. And when morn a-gain shall call us To run life's way,
   May we still, what-e'er be-fall us, Thy will o-bey.

From *New Music Horizons*, Book IV. Used by special permission of Silver Burdett Company, New York.

My Prayer

Florence Martin F.M.

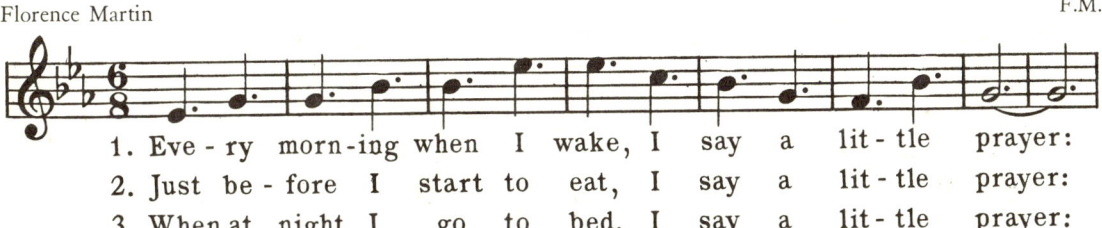
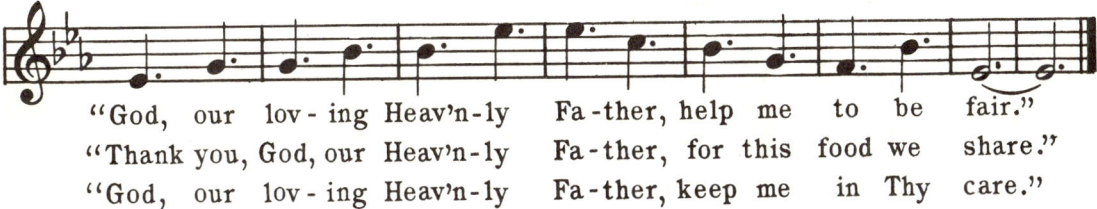

1. Eve-ry morn-ing when I wake, I say a lit-tle prayer:
   "God, our lov-ing Heav'n-ly Fa-ther, help me to be fair."
2. Just be-fore I start to eat, I say a lit-tle prayer:
   "Thank you, God, our Heav'n-ly Fa-ther, for this food we share."
3. When at night I go to bed, I say a lit-tle prayer:
   "God, our lov-ing Heav'n-ly Fa-ther, keep me in Thy care."

From *Father, Hear Thy Children Sing*, copyright 1953, by Hall & McCreary Company. Used by permission.

For Health and Strength

Round

For health and strength and dai-ly food, We praise Thy name, O Lord.

From *Singing Every Day* of Our Singing World, copyright, 1950. Used by permission of Ginn and Company, owner of the copyright.

Choral Grace

Emilie Fendall Johnson and Eleanor Graham — Johann Sebastian Bach

We thank Thee, Lord, for hap-py hearts, For rain and sun-ny weath-er.

We thank Thee, Lord, for this our food, And that we are to-geth-er.

Be with us, Lord, both night and day, And guide us in our work and play.

Words from *A Little Book of Prayers* by permission of the Viking Press. Copyright, 1941, by Emilie Fendall Johnson and Maud and Miska Petersham. Melody from *New Music Horizons*, Book III. Used by special permission of Silver Burdett Company, New York.

Thank Thee, Heav'nly Father

Florence Martin
Old French Melody Arranged by F.M.

From *Father, Hear Thy Children Sing*, copyright 1953, by Hall & McCreary Company. Used by permission.

Thank You, God

Jonath Battishiel
Ruth Heller

From *Father, Hear Thy Children Sing*, copyright 1953, by Hall & McCreary Company. Used by permission.

Hush, My Babe

Isaac Watts J. J. Rousseau

From *New Elementary Music,* by Charles A. Fullerton.

Slumber Song

Mabel E. Bray
Johann Sebastian Bach

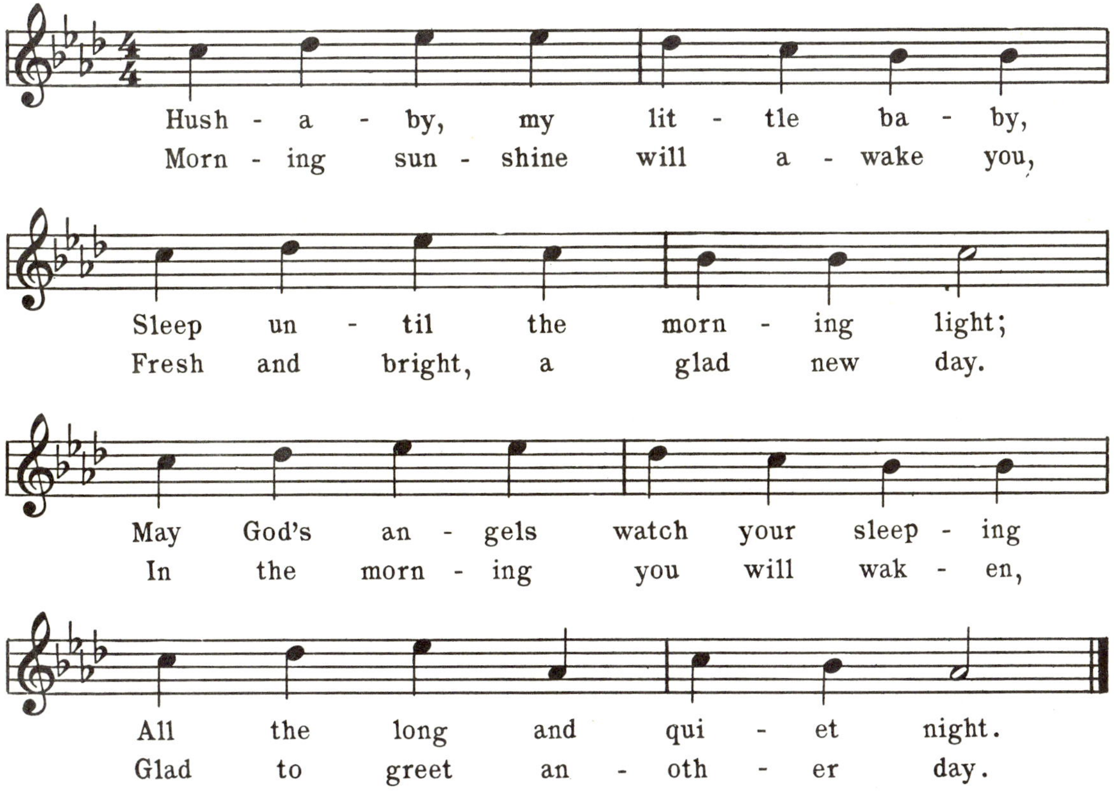

Hush - a - by, my lit - tle ba - by, Sleep un - til the morn - ing light; May God's an - gels watch your sleep - ing All the long and qui - et night.

Morn - ing sun - shine will a - wake you, Fresh and bright, a glad new day. In the morn - ing you will wak - en, Glad to greet an - oth - er day.

From *Music Hour*, Book I. Used by special permission of Silver Burdett Company, New York.

Index

First Lines and Titles

First lines of songs different from the titles appear in italics.

A

A Child's Evensong	151
A Child's Prayer (I)	46
A Child's Prayer (II)	53
A Child's Prayer (III)	103
A Child's Prayer (IV)	137
A Child's Prayer (V)	150
A Hymn of Thanks	136
Above the world the winter stars	35
All Creatures of Our God and King	26
All day long the shepherd	145
Alleluia! Easter Angels	91
All for Jesus, All for Jesus	103
All Glory, Laud and Honor	99
All praise to Thee, my God, this night	150
All the world is God's world	126
All Things Bright and Beautiful (First Tune)	22
All Things Bright and Beautiful (Second Tune)	23
All through the year we'll try to do	121
And God Said	19
An Evening Hymn	150
Another Year Is Dawning	35
Anywhere with Jesus	104
Apples mellow, Pumpkins yellow	32
A Prayer to Jesus	96
A Springtime Prayer	31
At the Dawn of Easter Day	91
Autumn	32
Away in a Manger (First Tune)	62
Away in a Manger (Second Tune)	63

B

Baby Jesus	61
Baby Jesus was born in Bethlehem	55
Bethlehem	57
Be to others ever kind	122
Blessed Lord of night and morning	135
Blow, winds, blow	29
Book Divine	106
Bright star of Christmas	71

C

Can a Little Child like Me?	44
Carol, Children, Carol	73
Chant thanksgiving, march along	18
Children's Chorale	130
Choral Grace	157
Christmas Carol	71
Christmas Chorale	65
Christ the Lord Is Ris'n Today	93
Closing Prayer	118
Come, We That Love the Lord	14
Come with Hearts Rejoicing	15
Cradled upon a Bed of Hay	66

D

Dare to Be a Daniel	108
Day Is Done	147
Day now is done	147
Dear Father, Bless Each Little Child	149
Dear Father, bless us as we go	118
Dear Father, hear the thanks that we bring	133
Dear little baby Moses	108

E

Each little flower that opens	22
Enter into His Gates	113
Evening	145
Evening Hymn	155
Evening Prayer	146
Evening shades are falling	145
Every morning when I wake	155

F

Fairest Lord Jesus	98
Faithful Is God	40
Father, as the morning sun	137
Father, Hear Thy Children Sing	48
Father, Hear Thy Little Children	141
Father in heaven, may Thy love guide us	140
Father, Lead Me Day by Day	52

Father, Teach Me	51
Father, We Bring Thee Our Praises	36
Father, we pray, Guard us today	139
Father, We Thank Thee (First Tune)	134
Father, We Thank Thee (Second Tune)	135
For a manger lowly	70
For all Thy tender mercies	133
For flow'rs that bloom about our feet	131
For flow'rs that bloom about our feet	30
For Health and Strength	157
For our home and daily food	158
For rain and sunshine and flowers bright and fair	42
For Stories Fine and True	106
For the Beauty of the Earth	49
For this new morning with its light	130
From the heav'n above us	151

G

Gladly lift we hearts and voices	41
Glory to God in the Highest	76
God Loves Me	36
God Made the Beautiful Sunshine	19
God Our Father Watch Will Keep	146
God Sees the Little Sparrow Fall	37
God's Gift of Day and Night	129
God's Love	143
God's Love Eternal	89
God's World	126
God, that madest earth and heaven	155
God Wants Us to Be Cheerful	124
God, who made the sun so bright	20
Go to sleep, O Child of mine	66
Gracious Saviour, Gentle Shepherd	87
Great Things	39

H

Happy Christmas Day	75
Happy Hearts	110
Happy Thought	27
Hear Our Prayer, O Lord	51
Heavenly Father	15
Heavenly Father, We Thy Children	117
Heav'nly Father, loving, tender	53
He Doeth All Things Well	20
Here in Our Father's House	114
Holy Bible, book divine!	106
Holy Spirit, come and stay	103
Home	121
Honor Thy Father and Mother	119

"Hosanna!" Be the Children's Song	100
How Lovely Are the Messengers	115
Hushaby, my little baby	161
Hush, My Babe	159

I

I am happy all day long	36
I am so glad that our Father in heav'n	82
I Give Thee My Hands	106
I like the cheerful summertime	32
I'm glad the golden sunlight	110
I'm very glad the spring has come	31
Infant So Gentle	76
In the early morning	129
In the morning when I waken	130
In the Temple	80
I Thank Thee, Lord, for Quiet Rest	136
I think when I read that sweet story of old	85
I've two little hands to work for Jesus	105
I Was Glad When They Said unto Me	110
I Will Sing to the Lord	13
I Would Follow Jesus	102

J

Jesus, from Thy Throne on High	94
Jesus Is the Friend of Children	83
Jesus Loves Even Me	82
Jesus Loves Me	81
Jesus, Tender Shepherd, Hear Me (First Tune)	153
Jesus, Tender Shepherd, Hear Me (Second Tune)	153
Jewels	95
Joy to the World	77

L

Let Me Learn of Jesus	87
Little Baby Jesus	61
Little Birds Are Gaily Singing	18
Little children, praise the Lord	113
Little Children, Praise the Saviour	100
Little drops of water	123
Little Moses	108
Little Things	123
Long ago the little children	84
Lord, I Would Own Thy Tender Care	47
Lord Jesus, may I always be	96
Lord of all things bright and fair	48
Lord, Teach a Little Child to Pray	52
Lord, that made the earth and air	136
Lord, Who Lovest Little Children	96
Love One Another	122

Lullaby to the Christ Child	67

M

Mary's Lullaby	66
May the Grace of Christ, Our Saviour	118
Morning Hymn (I)	131
Morning Hymn (II)	133
Morning Praise	142
Morning Prayer (I)	129
Morning Prayer (II)	133
Morning Prayer (III)	139
Morning Song	135
Mother's Day	121
My Jesus, I Love Thee	97
My Prayer	155

N

Now I Wake	139
Now Let Us All with One Accord	93
Now Let Your Happy Voices Ring	78
Now the day has come again	142
Now the Day Is Over	149
Now the Shades of Night Are Gone	141
Now the world is sleeping	146

O

O Come, Little Children	64
O Father, our dear Father	121
O God, I Thank Thee for Each Sight	138
O God, whose love enfolds us all	54
Oh, let the children everywhere	143
Oh, Worship the King	16
O Little Town of Bethlehem	58
On a bed of sweet, new hay	61
Once Again, Dear Lord, We Pray	126
Once upon a Hillside	84
On this happy day, happy Christmas day	75
Our Father, As We Start the Day	142
O, We, the Little Children	83

P

Praise and Thanks	38
Praise Him	42
Praise Him, Praise Him	14
Praise the Lord	113
Praise to God for Things We See	43
Praise to God, Immortal Praise	33
Prayer	140
Prayer for Each Day	137
Prayer for Peace	50

S

Saviour, Like a Shepherd Lead Us	88
See the Shining Dewdrops	29
Shepherds Leave the Hillside	67
Shepherds, Shake Off Your Drowsy Sleep	70
Silent Night	60
Sing to God	18
Sing to God in Joyful Voice	39
Sleep, my baby	67
Slumber Song	161
Smiles of Our Father	27
Soft the shadows round me creep	150
Standing by a purpose true	108
Stars Were Gleaming	69
Summertime	32

T

Teach Us to Pray	54
Tell Me the Stories of Jesus	86
Thank Him for work and play	41
Thanking God	41
Thanksgiving	128
Thanks to God	130
Thank Thee, Heav'nly Father	158
Thank you for the world so sweet	158
Thank You, God	158
Thank You, God, for All I Have	53
Thank You, God, for this new day	129
That Sweet Story of Old	85
The Bible Helps Me	107
The Children's Friend	84
The First Christmas Night	55
The Golden Rule	122
The Good Shepherd	145
The Holy Child	70
The hours of dark are past	137
The Lord hath done great things for us	39
The Many, Many Children	127
The Morning Bright	138
The Prayer of the Children	48
There Is a Green Hill Far Away	90
There Is a Happy Land	94
The world is so full of a number of things	27
This Is My Father's World	25
This Is the Day the Lord Hath Made	111
Thou Art with Us	41
Thou Holy Christ-Child, Blest and Dear	78
Thou, the Almighty	50
Thy Mercies, Lord	42

Thy Work, O God, Needs Many Hands	115
'Tis God Who Sends the Spring	31
To Thy Father and Thy Mother	119
True Neighbors	128
Two Little Hands	105

V

Very softly I will walk	111

W

We Are All God's Little Children	125
We Bring to Thee Our Offerings	117
We Give Thanks	47
Welcome, Holy Night	59
Welcome, thou holy, wonderful night	59
We Love Our Church, O God	114
We Pray for Children o'er the Sea	125
We pray to our Father	38
We're thankful for the springtime, Lord	31
We send our love to every land	128
We Thank Thee	30
We Thank Thee, Father, for Our Homes	45
We thank Thee, Lord, for happy hearts	157
We thank Thee, Lord, today	128
We Thank Thee, Loving Father	46
We thank Thee, loving Father	46
We thank Thee, O our Father	106
We Three Kings of Orient Are	74
We, Thy People, Praise Thee	16
When He cometh, when He cometh	95
When I Say My Prayer	154
When Jesus Was a Little Boy	79
When to Church I Go	111
Who Made the Pretty Lilies?	20
Winds through the olive trees	57
Wind, Sun, and Rain	29
Winter Song	35
Within yon lowly manger lies	65